بسم الله الرحمن الرحيم

TO THE READER

The reason why a special chapter is assigned to the collapse of the theory of evolution is that this theory constitutes the basis of all anti-spiritual philosophies. Since Darwinism rejects the fact of creation, and therefore the existence of God, during the last 140 years it has caused many people to abandon their faith or fall into doubt. Therefore, showing that this theory is a deception is a very important duty, which is strongly related to the religion (deen). It is imperative that this important service be rendered to everyone. Some of our readers may find the chance to read only one of our books. Therefore, we think it appropriate to spare a chapter for a summary of this subject.

In all the books by the author, faith-related issues are explained in the light of the Qur'anic verses and people are invited to learn God's words and to live by them. All the subjects that concern God's verses are explained in such a way as to leave no room for doubt or question marks in the reader's mind. The sincere, plain and fluent style employed ensures that everyone of every age and from every social group can easily understand the books. This effective and lucid narrative makes it possible to read them in a single sitting. Even those who rigorously reject spirituality are influenced by the facts recounted in these books and cannot refute the truthfulness of their contents.

This book and all the other works of the author can be read individually or discussed in a group at a time of conversation. Those readers who are willing to profit from the books will find discussion very useful in the sense that they will be able to relate their own reflections and experiences to one another.

In addition, it will be a great service to the religion to contribute to the presentation and reading of these books, which are written solely for the good pleasure of God. All the books of the author are extremely convincing. For this reason, for those who want to communicate the religion to other people, one of the most effective methods is to encourage them to read these books.

It is hoped that the reader will take time to look through the review of other books on the final pages of the book, and appreciate the rich source of material on faith-related issues, which are very useful
And a pleasure to read.

In these books, you will not find, as in some other books, the personal views of the author, explanations based on dubious sources, styles that are unobservant of the respect and reverence due to sacred subjects, nor hopeless, doubt-creating, and pessimistic accounts that create deviations in the heart.

BASIC TENETS OF ISLAM

Mankind! The truth has come to you from your Lord. Whoever is guided is only guided for his own good. Whoever is misguided is only misguided to his detriment. I have not been set over you as a guardian.
(Sura Yunus: 108)

HARUN YAHYA

September, 2002

© ALL RIGHTS RESERVED

BASIC TENETS OF ISLAM

HARUN YAHYA

Edited by: David Livingstone

ISBN No.: 81-7231-398-5

Edition: 2002

Published by Abdul Naeem for
Islamic Book Service
2241, Kucha Chelan, Darya Ganj,New Delhi - 110 002 (INDIA)
Ph.: 3253514, 3265380, 3286551,Fax: 3277913
E-mail: ibsdelhi@del2.vsnl.net.in & ibsdelhi@mantraonline.com
website: http://www.islamic-india.com

OUR ASSOCIATES
Islamic Book Service Inc.
136, Charlotte Ave., Hicksville, N.Y. 11801
Tel.: 516-8700-IBS (427), Fax: 516-8700-429
Toll Free: # 866-2424-IBS
E-mail: ibsny@conversent.net

Al Munna Book Shop Ltd.
P.O. Box-3449, Sharjah (U.A.E.), Tel.: 06-561-5483, 06-561-4650
E-mail: nusrat@emirates.net.ae
Branch: Dubai, Tel.: 04-3529294

Azhar Academy Ltd
AT Continenta (London) Ltd, Cooks Road London E15 2PW
Sales Hotline: 020 8534 9191, Fax: 020 8519 9190
E-mail: sales@azharacademy.org

Sartaj Company
P.O. Box-48535, Qualbert-4078, Durban, South Africa, Tel.: 305-3025
E-mail: sartaj@mweb.co.za

Printed at: **Noida Printing Press,** C-31, Sector 7, Noida (U.P.),Ph.: 91-4528211

All translations from the Qur'an are from "The Noble Qur'an: a New Rendering of its Meaning in English" by Hajj Abdalhaqq and Aisha Bewley, published by Bookwork, Norwich, UK. 1420 CE/1999 AH.

Website: http: // www.harunyahya.com
E-mail: info@harunyahya.com

About The Author

The author, who writes under the pen-name HARUN YAHYA, was born in Ankara in 1956. Having completed his primary and secondary education in Ankara, he then studied arts at Istanbul's Mimar Sinan University and philosophy at Istanbul University. Since the 1980s, the author has published many books on political, faith-related and scientific issues. Harun Yahya is well-known as an author who has written very important works disclosing the imposture of evolutionists, the invalidity of their claims and the dark liaisons between Darwinism and bloody ideologies.

His pen-name is made up of the names "Harun" (Aaron) and "Yahya" (John), in memory of the two esteemed prophets who fought against lack of faith. The Prophet's seal on the cover of the author's books has a symbolic meaning linked to the their contents. This seal represents the Qur'an as the last Book by God and the last word of Him and our Prophet, the last of all the prophets. Under the guidance of the Qur'an and Sunnah, the author makes it his main goal to disprove each one of the fundamental tenets of godless ideologies and to have the "last word", so as to completely silence the objections raised against religion. The seal of the Prophet, who attained ultimate wisdom and moral perfection, is used as a sign of his intention of saying this last word.

All these works by the author centre around one goal: to convey the message of the Qur'an to people, thus encouraging them to think about basic faith-related issues, such as the existence of God, His unity and the hereafter, and to display the decrepit foundations and perverted works of godless systems. Harun Yahya enjoys a wide readership in many countries, from India to America, England to Indonesia, Poland to Bosnia, and Spain to Brazil. Some of his books are available in English, French, German, Italian, Portuguese, Urdu, Arabic, Albanian, Russian, Serbo-Croat (Bosnian), Uygur Turkish, and Indonesian, and they have been enjoyed by readers all over the world.

Greatly appreciated all around the world, these works have been instrumental in many people putting their faith in God and in many others gaining a deeper insight into their faith. The wisdom, and the sincere and easy-to-understand style employed give these books a distinct touch which directly strikes any one who reads or examines them. Immune to objections, these works are characterised by their features of rapid effectiveness, definite results and irrefutability. It is unlikely that those who read these books and give a serious thought to them can any longer sincerely advocate the materialistic philosophy, atheism and any other perverted ideology or philosophy. Even if they continue to advocate, this will be only a sentimental insistence since these books have refuted these ideologies from their very basis. All contemporary movements of denial are ideologically defeated today, thanks to the collection of books written by Harun Yahya.

There is no doubt that these features result from the wisdom and lucidity of the Qur'an. The author certainly does not feel proud of himself; he merely intends to serve as a means in one's search for God's right path. Furthermore, no material gain is sought in the publication of these works.

Considering these facts, those who encourage people to read these books, which open the "eyes" of the heart and guide them in becoming more devoted servants of God, render an invaluable service.

Meanwhile, it would just be a waste of time and energy to propagate books which create confusion in peoples' minds, lead man into ideological chaos, and which, clearly have no strong and precise effects in removing the doubts in peoples' hearts, as also verified from previous experience. It is apparent that it is impossible for books devised to emphasize the author's literary power rather than the noble goal of saving people from loss of faith, to have such a great effect. Those who doubt this can readily see that the sole aim of Harun Yahya's books is to overcome disbelief and to disseminate the moral values of the Qur'an. The success, impact and sincerity this service has attained are manifest in the reader's conviction.

One point needs to be kept in mind: The main reason for the continuing cruelty and conflict, and all the ordeals Muslims undergo is the ideological prevalence of disbelief. These things can only come to an end with the ideological defeat of disbelief and by ensuring that everybody knows about the wonders of creation and Qur'anic morality, so that people can live by it. Considering the state of the world today, which forces people into the downward spiral of violence, corruption and conflict, it is clear that this service has to be provided more speedily and effectively. Otherwise, it may be too late.

It is no exaggeration to say that the collection of books by Harun Yahya have assumed this leading role. By the Will of God, these books will be the means through which people in the 21st century will attain the peace and bliss, justice and happiness promised in the Qur'an.

The works of the author include *The New Masonic Order, Judaism and Freemasonry, The Disasters Darwinism Brought to Humanity, Communism in Ambush, The Bloody Ideology of Darwinism: Fascism, The 'Secret Hand' in Bosnia, Behind the Scenes of The Holocaust, Behind the Scenes of Terrorism, Israel's Kurdish Card, Solution: The Morals of the Qur'an, Articles 1-2-3, A Weapon of Satan: Romantism, Truths 1-2, The Western World Turns to God, The Evolution Deceit, Precise Answers to Evolutionists, Evolutionary Falsehoods, Perished Nations, For Men of Understanding, The Prophet Moses, The Prophet Joseph, The Golden Age, Allah's Artistry in Colour, Glory is Everywhere, The Truth of the Life of This World, Knowing the Truth, Eternity Has Already Begun, Timelessness and the Reality of Fate, The Dark Magic of Darwinism, The Religion of Darwinism, The Collapse of the Theory of Evolution in 20 Questions, Allah is Known Through Reason, The Qur'an Leads the Way to Science, The Real Origin of Life, Consciousness in the Cell, A String of Miracles, The Creation of the*

Universe, Miracles of the Qur'an, The Design in Nature, Self-Sacrifice and Intelligent Behaviour Models in Animals, The End of Darwinism, Deep Thinking, Never Plead Ignorance, The Green Miracle Photosynthesis, The Miracle in the Cell, The Miracle in the Eye, The Miracle in the Spider, The Miracle in the Gnat, The Miracle in the Ant, The Miracle of the Immune System, The Miracle of Creation in Plants, The Miracle in the Atom, The Miracle in the Honeybee, The Miracle of Seed, The Miracle of Hormone, The Miracle of the Termite, The Miracle of the Human Being, The Miracle of Man's Creation, The Miracle of Protein, The Secrets of DNA.

The author's childrens books are: *Children Darwin Was Lying!*, *The World of Animals*, *The Splendour in the Skies*, *The World of Our Little Friends: The Ants*, *Honeybees That Build Perfect Combs*, *Skillful Dam Builders: Beavers*.

The author's other works on Quranic topics include: *The Basic Concepts in the Qur'an, The Moral Values of the Qur'an, Quick Grasp of Faith 1-2-3, Ever Thought About the Truth?, Crude Understanding of Disbelief, Devoted to Allah, Abandoning the Society of Ignorance, The Real Home of Believers: Paradise, Knowledge of the Qur'an, Qur'an Index, Emigrating for the Cause of Allah, The Character of the Hypocrite in the Qur'an, The Secrets of the Hypocrite, The Names of Allah, Communicating the Message and Disputing in the Qur'an, Answers from the Qur'an, Death Resurrection Hell, The Struggle of the Messengers, The Avowed Enemy of Man: Satan, The Greatest Slander: Idolatry, The Religion of the Ignorant, The Arrogance of Satan, Prayer in the Qur'an, The Importance of Conscience in the Qur'an, The Day of Resurrection, Never Forget, Disregarded Judgements of the Qur'an, Human Characters in the Society of Ignorance, The Importance of Patience in the Qur'an, General Information from the Qur'an, The Mature Faith, Before You Regret, Our Messengers Say, The Mercy of Believers, The Fear of Allah, The Nightmare of Disbelief, Jesus Will Return, Beauties Presented by the Qur'an for Life, A Bouquet of the Beauties of Allah 1-2-3-4, The Iniquity Called "Mockery", The Mystery of the Test, The True Wisdom According to the Qur'an, The Struggle with the Religion of Irreligion, The School of Yusuf, The Alliance of the Good, Slanders Spread Against Muslims Throughout History, The Importance of Following the Good Word, Why Do You Deceive Yourself?, Islam: The Religion of Ease, Enthusiasm and Excitement in the Qur'an, Seeing Good in Everything, How do the Unwise Interpret the Qur'an?, Some Secrets of the Qur'an, The Courage of Believers, Being Hopeful in the Qur'an, Justice and Tolerance in the Qur'an, Basic Tenets of Islam, Those Who do not Listen to the Qur'an.*

CONTENTS

PREFACE	11
THERE IS NO GOD BUT HIM	13
GOD ENCOMPASSES EVERYTHING	16
GOD IS NEAR TO MAN	17
GOD CREATED EVERYTHING ACCORDING TO A FIXED DECREE	18
GOD HAS POWER OVER EVERYTHING	19
GOD SEES AND KNOWS EVERYTHING	22
ALL BEINGS ARE SUBJECTED TO GOD	24
FALSE BELIEFS ABOUT GOD	26
FAITH IN GOD FREE OF IDOLATRY	29
ASSESSING GOD WITH A JUST ASSESSMENT	31
GOD'S INFINITE GREATNESS AND POWER	32
LOVE OF GOD AND FEAR OF GOD	36
THE QUR'AN IS A GUIDE	40
BELIEF IN THE BOOKS REVEALED BY GOD AND BELIEF IN HIS MESSENGERS	42
FAITH IN THE ANGELS	43
THE TEMPORARY NATURE OF THE LIFE OF THIS WORLD	44
MAN IS BEING TESTED	47
DEATH IS NOT THE END	50
BELIEF IN THE HEREAFTER	53
FAITH IN THE DAY OF JUDGEMENT	55
THE RESURRECTION	58
THE DAY OF JUDGEMENT	60
PARADISE AND HELL	62
THE AIM IS TO ATTAIN THE GOOD PLEASURE OF GOD	67
SIN AND REPENTANCE	69
RELIGION IS IN CONFORMITY WITH NATURAL INCLINATION OF MANKIND	71
BELIEVERS MUST BE TOGETHER AND COOPERATE	76
THE LAST WORD	79
THE MISCONCEPTION OF EVOLUTION	80

PREFACE

This book is written for those who have recently been introduced to Islam, and who already have knowledge and some degree of conviction about Islam, but which may have had their origin in inadequate or invalid sources. The information people gather about Islam is, in most cases, limited to what their families, friends or certain books present. However, accurate information about Islam can be accessed only by referring to the Qur'an, the source of Islam.

The Qur'an is the final revelation sent by God, as guidance to mankind. While the Torah and the Gospel, the two holy books preceding the Qur'an, were also revelations from God, in time, they were distorted and lost their quality as the divine word of God. Although they may contain parts of the original word of God, their greater part consists of words and interpolations of man. The only book revealed by God to have survived completely intact, is the Qur'an. It contains only that which has been revealed by God. God sent down His message, either by way of Gabriel, or through direct inspiration to the Prophet Muhammad (Pbuh). The Qur'an consists of only that which was revealed to the Prophet Muhammad (Pbuh), sent down in stages through the agency of Gabriel for a period of twenty-three years.

At every state, the revelation was immediately recorded in writing, or committed to memory, by the Prophet (Pbuh) and his companions. Today, all Muslims wherever they are, read the same

Qur'an. No contradiction or discrepancy can be found in any of the copies. (In our day, the Qur'an of Uthman, the third Caliph, is displayed in Topkapi Museum, Istanbul.) Evidence that the Qur'an is from God is the total absence of any sort of contradiction in the Qur'an. According to the Book of God:

Will they not ponder the Qur'an? If it had been from other than God, they would have found many inconsistencies in it. (Sura an-Nisa': 82)

The Qur'an is guidance to lead man to the path of rectitude. It is the revelation of God, sent to bring man from darkness to light. By way of the Qur'an, Our Lord, the Creator of man and all living things, directs His servants to the Straight Path. In a verse, God states:

Mankind! Admonition has come to you from your Lord and also healing for what is in the breasts and guidance and mercy for the believers. (Sura Yunus: 57)

God's existence, His unity, the signs of creation, and the life of the hereafter, are those basic facts most stressed in the Qur'an. In many verses of the Qur'an, God invites man to think and to ponder on the divine wisdom in God's creation, and on the transience of the life of this world, and the permanence of the life of the hereafter. As well, we can also find in the Qur'an, accounts of the lives of the prophets; their sincerity in faith, their commitment to God's cause, and their determination in spreading the divine message. Finally, a number of verses in the Qur'an also provide us with insight into how we should conduct ourselves in our everyday lives.

In this book, based on information provided by the Qur'an, we will discuss God, His attributes, the real purpose of our existence in this world, what we need to do to comply with it, the reality of death and that which awaits us, the afterlife.

We highly recommend that you read this book carefully, and reflect upon its lessons, because they are intended to draw you nearer to your Creator, and show you the way to infinite bliss and salvation.

THERE IS NO GOD BUT HIM

The essence of Islam is to know of the existence of God, and to understand that there is no god but Him. To practice Islam is to allow this truth to manifest itself in every aspect of one's life. According to the Qur'an:

Your God is One God. There is no god but Him, the All-Merciful, the Most Merciful. (Sura al-Baqara: 163)

Most people think that matter, the underlying substance of the universe, has an absolute existence, and regard God as but an abstract idea. (God is truly beyond what they ascribe to Him.) The truth is, however, only God truly exists, and the rest is merely His creation.

The entire universe and everything in it was created by God. Before the creation of the universe, nothing existed, in the material sense. It was all non-existence. At the moment when the universe was created, the Al-Awwal (The First) and Al-Akhir (The Last) God, Who is unbounded by time and space, created time, matter and space. The Qur'an relates this matter as follows:

The Originator of the heavens and earth. When He decides on something, He just says to it, "Be!" and it is. (Sura al-Baqara: 117)

Contrary to the perceived wisdom, God did not create matter and then leave it on its own. Everything happening, even at this very instant, is ordained by God. Every raindrop, each child that opens its eyes to the world, the process of photosynthesis in plants, all the bodily functions of living things, the courses of stars in far remote galaxies, each seed sprouting forth, or any other event that we might think of, or fail to think of, are all ordained by God. It is God Who creates all things. Every event occurs within His command:

> It is God Who created the seven heavens and of the earth the ame number, the Command descending down through all of them, so that you might know that God has power over all things and that God encompasses all things in His knowledge. (Sura at-Talaq: 12)
>
> He Who originates creation and then regenerates it and provides for you from out of heaven and earth. Is there another god besides God? Say: "Bring your proof if you are being truthful." (Sura an-Naml: 64)

Were the universe left to its own will, it would become disordered, scattered and corrupted. However, the perfect equilibrium in all things, from the cells of a living organism, to the stars in deep outer space, all reveal the existence of something that is controlling them at every moment, with the same perfection as their original creation. In any corner of the universe, one will always come to recognize a flawless plan:

> He Who created the seven heavens in layers. You will not find any flaw in the creation of the All-Merciful. Look again— do you see any gaps? Then look again and again. Your sight will return to you dazzled and exhausted! (Sura al-Mulk: 3-4)

Denying that God is the Creator, and attributing divinity to that which He created, despite the abundance of proof to the contrary, is as nonsensical as claiming that a skyscraper was not built by construction workers, but came into being by the free will of bricks, or the placement of one on top of the other by pure coincidence.

The perfect order in the universe, and the supreme design of living things, reveals to us that they must have all been created by a single Creator. If there were other gods, that is, others capable of similarly ordaining their will, disorder and confusion would prevail. That there is no god but Him, and that no other being in the universe has any similar power, is related in a verse of the Qur'an as follows:

God has no son and there is no other god accompanying Him, for then each god would have gone off with what he created and one of them would have been exalted above the other. Glory be to God above what they describe.
(Sura al-Muminun: 91)

In the supplication below, the Prophet Muhammad (Pbuh) stressed that there is no deity but God and a believer has to turn to Him in all matters:

None has the right to be worshipped but God, the Majestic, the Most Forbearing. None has the right to be worshipped but God, the Lord of the Tremendous Throne. None has the right to be worshipped but God, the Lord of the Heavens and the Lord of the Honourable Throne. (Al-Bukhari)

As stressed above, there is no other god besides Him. He has no son. He is above such human attributes. We clearly understand from the verse below that those religions claiming that God has a "son" are misguided. The Oneness of God is further emphasized in the Qur'an as follows:

> Say: "He is God, Absolute Oneness, God, the Everlasting Sustainer of all. He has not given birth and was not born. And no one is comparable to Him." (Sura al-Ikhlas: 1-4)

GOD ENCOMPASSES EVERYTHING

Some people think that God is found in a certain place. The belief that God is up in the sky, in a remote corner of the universe, is held by many people. The fact is, however, that God is anywhere, encompassing everything. He is the actual and the only absolute being, to Whom all beings are subjected:

> God, there is no god but Him, the Living, the Self-Sustaining. He is not subject to drowsiness or sleep. Everything in the heavens and the earth belongs to Him. Who can intercede with Him except by His permission? He knows what is before them and what is behind them but they cannot grasp any of His knowledge save what He wills. His Footstool encompasses the heavens and the earth and their preservation does not tire Him. He is the Most High, the Magnificent. (Sura al-Baqara: 255)

God has everything within His grasp at any given moment. There is no creature He does not hold by the forelock. He has power over all things and is exalted high above any weakness or inability.

GOD IS NEAR TO MAN

Many people think God is far away. However, as stated in the Qur'an, "...**Surely your Lord encompasses the people with His knowledge...**" (Sura al-Isra': 60), He is very near. He sees and knows every aspect of a human being, and hears every word man utters. He is knowledgeable of even one's inner thoughts. This is related in the Qur'an as follows:

We created man and We know what his own self whispers to him. We are nearer to him than his jugular vein. (Sura Qaf: 16)

God is so near to man that He hears the prayer of everyone–even if he prays inwardly–and it is He Who answers it:

If My servants ask you about Me, I am near. I answer the call of the caller when he calls on Me. They should therefore respond to Me and believe in Me so that hopefully they will be rightly guided. (Sura al-Baqara: 186)

God knows what a person harbours in his heart. He knows whether he engages in a deed to earn His consent, or to satisfy his own lower soul. God reminds us that He knows our inner thoughts:

...Know that God knows what is in your selves, so beware of Him! And know that God is Ever-Forgiving, All-Forbearing. (Sura al-Baqara: 235)

Though you speak out loud, He knows your secrets and what is even more concealed. (Sura Ta Ha: 7)

God's Messenger, the Prophet Muhammad (Pbuh) also reminded Muslims when they prayed that God is very close to them by saying, *"You are calling a Hearer, One very close by; The One*

Who you are calling is closer to each one of you."(Al-Bukhari and Muslim)

As He is with you at every moment, God is with you as you are reading this book; He sees what you are doing and knows what you are thinking. This fact is related in the Qur'an as follows:

Do you not see that God knows what is in the heavens and on the earth? Three men cannot confer together secretly without Him being the fourth of them, or five without Him being the sixth of them, or fewer than that or more without Him being with them wherever they are. Then He will inform them on the Day of Rising of what they did. God has knowledge of all things. (Sura al-Mujadala: 7)

GOD CREATED EVERYTHING ACCORDING TO A FIXED DECREE

We have created all things according to a fixed decree. (Sura al-Qamar: 49)

Destiny is part of God's perfect creation and all events, past and future, are known to Him as in a timeless "single moment."

It is God Who created matter. What we call time is the motion of matter. Time is a dimension which is relative only to man. Only man perceives the passage of time; a human being can recognize his own existence only as it exists in time. God, however, is not bound by time, for it is He Who created it. In other words, God is independent of the flow of time; God does not need to wait to see what will happen in the future. God is truly exalted above all such deficiencies. God knows of a future event (future for us) before it happens, because God, the First and the Last, is not bound by time, and because He is the Absolute and the Infinite. Not bound by time, God is aware of an event which, from our perspective, will take place thousands of years later. In fact, it is He Who willed, determined and created it. This truth is revealed in a verse as follows:

> **Nothing occurs, either in the earth or in yourselves, without its being in a Book before We make it happen. That is something easy for God. (Sura al-Hadid: 22)**

GOD HAS POWER OVER EVERYTHING

God, the Creator of everything, is the sole possessor of all beings. It is God Who heaps up the heavy clouds, heats and brightens the earth, varies the direction of the winds, holds birds suspended up in the sky, splits the seed, makes a man's heart beat, ordains photosynthesis in plants, and keeps planets in their separate orbits. People generally surmise that such phenomena occur according to "the laws of physics," "gravity," "aerodynamics," or other physical factors; however, there is one point these people ignore: all such physical laws were created by God. In fact, the only possessor of power in the universe is God.

God rules all the systems in the universe, regardless of whether we are aware of them, or if we are asleep, sitting, walking. Each of the myriad of processes in the universe, all essential to our existence, is under God's control. Even our ability to just take a small step forward depends on countless minutely predetermined details, including earth's force of gravity, the structure of the human skeleton, the nervous system and muscular system, the brain, the heart, and even the rotation speed of the earth.

Attributing the existence of the world and of the entire universe to sheer coincidence is complete delusion. The exquisite order of the earth and the universe completely contradicts the possibility of formation through coincidence, and is, rather, a clear sign of God's infinite might. For instance, the earth's orbit around the sun deviates only 2.8 mm in every 29 kms from the right path. If this deviation were 0.3 mm longer or shorter, then living beings all over the earth would either freeze or be scorched. While it is virtually impossible for even a marble to revolve in the same orbit without any deviation, the earth accomplishes such a course despite its gigantic mass. As stated in the Qur'an, **"...God has appointed a measure for all things..."** (Sura at-Talaq: 3). In effect, the splendid order in the universe is maintained as a result of fantastic systems that depend on highly delicate equilibriums.

Many hold the perverted belief that God "created everything and then left them on their own." However, any event, taking place in any area of the universe, occurs solely by God's Will, and under His control. The Qur'an states the following:

Do you not know that God knows everything in heaven and earth? That is in a Book. That is easy for God. (Sura al-Hajj: 70)

It is very important to grasp this fact for someone who strives to come near to God. The prayer of Prophet Muhammad (Pbuh) quoted below is a very good example of this:

O God: All the Praises are for You: You are the Lord of the Heavens and the Earth. All the Praises are for You; You are the Maintainer of the Heaven and the Earth and whatever is in them. All the Praises are for You; You are the Light of the Heavens and the Earth. Your Word is the Truth, and Your Promise is the Truth, and the Meeting with You is the Truth, and Paradise is the Truth, and the (Hell) Fire is the Truth, and the Hour is the Truth. O God! I surrender myself to You, and I believe in You and I depend upon You, and I repent to You and with You (Your evidences) I stand against my opponents, and to you I leave the judgment (for those who refuse my message). O God! Forgive me my sins that I did in the past or will do in the future, and also the sins I did in secret or in public. You are my only God (Whom I worship) and there is no other God for me (i.e. I worship none but You). (Al-Bukhari)

Elaborate processes taking place in the bodies of living things are impressive examples that help us to grasp God's might. For instance, at every moment, your kidneys filter your blood and extricate those harmful molecules to be excreted from the body. This screening and elimination process, which can be carried out by a single kidney cell, can only be accomplished by a giant haemodialyser (artificial kidney). A haemodialyser was consciously designed by scientists. A kidney, however, does not sense, or have a decision-making centre, nor the faculty of thought. In other words, an unconscious kidney cell can accomplish tasks that otherwise demand an elaborate thinking process.

It is possible to encounter millions of such examples in living beings. Molecules, composed of unconscious matter, perform tasks so remarkable they would otherwise suggest consciousness. The consciousness apparent in these cases though is, of course, of God's infinite wisdom and knowledge. It is God Who designed the kidney cells, as well as the molecules discussed, and Who orders them to accomplish their respective tasks. In the Qur'an, God informs us that He constantly sends down "commands" to the beings He created:

> **It is God Who created the seven heavens and of the earth the same number, the Command descending down through all of them, so that you might know that God has power over all things and that God encompasses all things in His knowledge. (Sura at-Talaq: 12)**

Clearly, God, Who created everything in the universe, is surely able to bring the dead to life. Of this fact, God states the following:

> **Do they not see that God–He Who created the heavens and the earth and was not wearied by creating them–has the power to bring the dead to life? Yes indeed! He has power over all things. (Sura al-Ahqaf: 33)**

GOD SEES AND KNOWS EVERYTHING

People cannot see God–unless He wills–, being the main reason why so many often falsely presume that God cannot see them (truly, God is far above that which they ascribe to Him). God sees and knows all things, down to the minutest detail, as indicated in a verse of the Qur'an as follows:

> **Eyesight cannot perceive Him but He perceives eyesight. He is the All-Penetrating, the All-Aware. (Sura al-An'am: 103)**

Wherever a person may be, God is surely with him. Right at this moment, as you are reading these lines, God sees you and knows exactly what crosses your mind. Wherever you go, or whatever you do, this is always the case. As the Qur'an explains:

You do not engage in any matter or recite any part of the Qur'an or do any action without Our witnessing you while you are occupied with it. Not even the smallest speck eludes your Lord, either on earth or in heaven. Nor is there anything smaller than that, or larger, which is not in a Clear Book. (Sura Yunus: 61)

It is He Who created the heavens and the earth in six days, then established Himself firmly on the Throne. He knows what goes into the earth and what comes out of it, what comes down from heaven and what goes up into it. He is with you wherever you are—God sees what you do. (Sura al-Hadid: 4)

The Prophet Muhammad (Pbuh) also reminded believers to keep this in mind when he said, *"God is above the Throne and nothing is hidden from God of your deeds."*

Aware of this fact, a believer submits himself to his Lord, seeks refuge in Him, and fears nothing but Him. God's command to Prophet Moses, and Aaron, who hesitated in going to Pharaoh to summon him to Islam, is a lesson for all believers:

He said, "Have no fear. I will be with you, All-Hearing and All-Seeing." (Sura Ta Ha: 46)

ALL BEINGS ARE SUBJECTED TO GOD

All beings in the universe, either living or non-living, are under God's command. They can act only if He wills. They can only perform those tasks which He wills. For example, honeybees, who produce more honey than their actual need, could not possibly know that honey is beneficial to humans; nor could they be aware of the precise chemical composition that makes it so useful and delicious. In fact, in addition to not knowing why they produce an abundance of much honey, nor could they possess the intelligence to construct the orderly hexagonal honeycombs, each of which is a miracle of design and mathematics. It is God, to Whom all beings are subjected, that causes bees accomplish these feats. That bees act in compliance with God's command is related in the Qur'an as follows:

> **Your Lord revealed to the bees: "Build dwellings in the mountains and the trees, and also in the structures which men erect. Then eat from every kind of fruit and travel the paths of your Lord, which have been made easy for you to follow" From inside them comes a drink of varying colours, containing healing for mankind. There is certainly a Sign in that for people who reflect. (Sura an-Nahl: 68-69)**

Bees' compliance with God's commands in the manner in which they conduct themselves is not an anomaly. God provides us with this example to allow us to understand that all beings, including man, act by His Will. The Qur'an indicates that this is a sign for those who reflect. All beings are entirely subjected to His command:

All Beings Are Subjected To God

Everyone in the heavens and earth belongs to Him. All are submissive to Him. (Sura ar-Rum: 26)

Some religions consider Satan to be a being apart from and independent of God. Some attribute individual power to Satan. However, both opinions are incorrect. Satan, as well as the disbelievers who follow him, are subjected to God's Will. God created Satan to put man to test, and endowed him with the ability and authority to call mankind to disbelief. God's address to Satan is related in the Qur'an:

> He (God) said, "Get out! you accursed!
> My curse is upon you until the Day of Reckoning."
> He (Satan) said, "My Lord, grant me a reprieve until the Day they are raised again." He said, "You are among the reprieved until the Day whose time is known."
> He said, "By Your might, I will mislead all of them
> except for Your chosen servants among them."
> He said, "By the truth—and I speak the truth—
> I will fill up Hell with you and every one of them who follows you." (Sura Sâd: 77-85)

Just as man is, Satan is also entirely under God's control, and subjected to His Will. He is not a being possessing a will apart from and independent of God; he can neither make such decisions nor carry them out. In the trial set for human beings in this life, he is merely a being that is expected to distinguish the righteous from the corrupt.

FALSE BELIEFS ABOUT GOD

The Torah and the Gospel, the earlier revelations from God, have lost their original authenticity, since the words and interpolations of man have been incorporated into them. This is one of the reasons for which the Qur'an was sent. That the holy books which preceded the Qur'an were distorted by man is related by God as follows:

> Woe to those who write the Book with their own hands and then say "This is from God" to sell it for a paltry price. Woe to them for what their hands have written! Woe to them for what they earn! (Sura Al-Baqara: 79)

> Among them is a group who distort the Book with their tongues so that you think it is from the Book when it is not from the Book. They say, "It is from God," but it is not from God. They tell a lie against God and they know it.
> (Sura Al 'Imran: 78)

Distortion of the Torah and the Gospel led proliferation of false beliefs among their adherents. These holy books include beliefs and ideas that derive from outside of God's true religion. This manifests itself in the distortion of the true revelation, and the depiction of God as a being with weaknesses and imperfections peculiar to human beings. (Truly, God is above what they ascribe to Him).

In the corrupted Torah, for instance, a story has been fabricated in which God is depicted as a being who was defeated in wrestling bout with the Prophet Jacob (May be in peace). Similarly, in another tale, it is claimed that having created the world in six days,

False Beliefs About God

God became weary and rested on the seventh day. However, God, being exalted far above any imperfections, cannot become weary or in need of rest. This is related in the Qur'an as follows:

We created the heavens and the earth, and everything between them, in six days and We were not affected by fatigue. (Sura Qaf: 38)

Do they not see that God—He Who created the heavens and the earth and was not wearied by creating them—has the power to bring the dead to life? Yes indeed! He has power over all things. (Sura al-Ahqaf: 33)

This reveals that the adherents of these books have swerved from the straight path, and have not had an accurate understanding of God and His attributes.

The Qur'an, on the other hand, is under God's protection, and is the only book revealed by God to have survived intact. The Qur'an is the book of Islam, the only true religion:

It is We Who have sent down the Reminder and We Who will preserve it. (Sura al-Hijr: 9)

If anyone desires anything other than Islam as a religion, it will not be accepted from him, and in the hereafter he will be among the losers. (Sura Al 'Imran: 85)

The Qur'an refers to the erroneous beliefs adopted by Christians and Jews, and makes known the correct belief. For instance, their saying, "God has a son (Jesus)," which is one of the tenets of Christianity, is said to be merely an irrational belief and a lie said against God:

They say, "God has a son." Glory be to Him! No, everything in the heavens and earth belongs to Him. Everything is obedient to Him, the Originator of the heavens and earth.

When He decides on something, He just says to it, "Be!" and it is. (Sura al-Baqara: 116-117)

Some other verses related to this matter are as follows:

People of the Book! Do not go to excess in your religion. Say nothing but the truth about God. The Messiah, Jesus the son of Mary, was only the Messenger of God and His Word, which He cast into Mary, and a Spirit from Him. So believe in God and His Messengers. Do not say, "Three." It is better that you stop. God is only One God. He is too Glorious to have a son! Everything in the heavens and in the earth belongs to Him. God suffices as a Guardian. (Sura An-Nisa': 171)

He is the Originator of the heavens and the earth. How could He have a son when He has no wife? He created all things and He has knowledge of all things. (Sura al-An'am: 101)

Christian belief maintains that God created the universe and then left it to its own. Yet, as stated earlier, God commands Will over the universe at every single moment; it is constantly within His control. Nothing can happen without His Will and control:

He Who originates creation and then regenerates it and provides for you from out of heaven and earth. Is there another god besides God? Say: "Bring your proof if you are being truthful." (Sura an-Naml: 64)

God keeps a firm hold on the heavens and earth, preventing them from vanishing away. And if they vanished no one could then keep hold of them. Certainly He is Most Forbearing, Ever-Forgiving. (Sura Fatir: 41)

To counter these false notions, and many others not mentioned here, God gives His sublime attributes for us in the Qur'an. This is in order to, not only answer these erroneous claims, but also to guide those guilty of them to the true religion of God.

Everyone must acknowledge that God is One, and that nothing is comparable to Him; He is free of any weakness. He encompasses everything, He exercises His command over creation at every moment, He is near to man, He has the power to do anything, He is the Most Merciful, He is the Just, He is the King of the Day of Judgement, He sees and hears everything, and is the most sublime in attributes.

FAITH IN GOD FREE OF IDOLATRY

Have you seen him who has taken his whims and desires to be his god? Will you then be his guardian? (Sura al-Furqan: 43)

"Shirk", the word used for idolatry in Arabic means "partnership/association." In the Qur'an, it refers to ascribing associates to God, or deeming someone or something, called idols or false-gods, worthy of worship beside or in addition to God. Idolatry, though, is not limited to worshipping totems or non-living beings. Because, man's responsibility is to serve his Creator, and to strive to earn His good pleasure alone, his pursuit of any other goal is to ascribe worship to something other than God. For instance, a person would be guilty of idolatry if he were to seek the pleasure of people instead of God's. Likewise, it would again be ascribing associates to God if one's purpose in life is to satisfy his whims and desires rather than to earn God's good pleasure. Many people ascribe divinity to things like money, status, wealth and so on.

The Qur'an refers to idolaters of Arab society, who set aside a portion of their crops and cattle for their idols, as follows:

They assign to God a share of the crops and livestock He has created, saying, "This is for God,"–as they allege–"and this is for our idols." Their idols' share does not reach God whereas God's share reaches their idols! What an evil judgement they make! (Sura al-An'am: 136)

As is mentioned in the verse above, idolaters assign a part of their wealth to God, and another part to their idols. This is characteristic of the delusion of idolaters.

Loving a being more than God or loving him/it as one ought to love God is again a form of idolatry. Similarly, someone who fears a being as he should fear God, idolizes it, since he assumes that being possesses a might apart from and independent of God.

Muslims, however, firmly believe that everything is created by God, that all affairs are regulated by Him, that causes do not have any power to produce a result independently, that every event is predetermined and created by God, that God is the possessor of the ultimate will and judgement. This is the kind of belief system that God reveals to us in the Qur'an. Deviation from these tenets, believing that everything occurs spontaneously, as the result of coincidences, attributing the power to create to some other causes, are all forms of ascribing associates to God. God does not forgive idolatry:

> **God does not forgive anything being associated with Him but He forgives whoever He wills for anything other than that. Anyone who associates something with God has gone very far astray. (Sura an-Nisa': 116)**

When God's Messenger (Pbuh) was asked, *"What is the biggest sin in the sight of God?"*, he said, *"To set up rivals unto God although He alone created you."* (Al-Bukhari)

ASSESSING GOD WITH A JUST ASSESSMENT

They do not measure God with His true measure. God is All-Strong, Almighty. (Sura Al-Hajj: 74)

God manifests His infinite might and knowledge everywhere. The perfection of every part of the human body, the knowledge in the design of a flower, the beauty in its colour and scent, the glory in the heavens and the universe, the order in the orbits of the planets, the fish in the depths of oceans, and the intricate design in everything you see around, are all clear manifestations of God's infiniteness and power. Some disbelievers, despite perceiving God's existence and His infinite might, deny Him out of arrogance. They do not acknowledge God's true greatness. Because they lack wisdom, they fail to see the evident signs of God's existence and of His greatness manifested in all beings. The inattention of these people is expressed in a verse as follows:

How many Signs there are in the heavens and earth! Yet they pass them by, turning away from them. (Sura Yusuf: 105)

Only those who reflect on the purpose of the creation around them, who have a clear faculty of discernment, who apply their minds and use their conscience, can recognize the truth that which these signs imply. They are those who believe. One of the primary attributes of a believer is his ability to be perceptive. Believers, who are capable of exercising their minds, unencumbered by false motives, come to recognize God's artistry and power through His creation, and thus have a full appreciation of His greatness and glory. A verse of the Qur'an relates that those who are able to think clearly see God's signs wherever they turn:

In the creation of the heavens and earth, and the alternation of the night and day, and the ships which sail the seas to people's benefit, and the water which God sends down from the sky—by which He brings the earth to life when it was dead and scatters about in it creatures of every kind—and the varying direction of the winds, and the clouds subservient between heaven and earth, there are Signs for people who use their intellect. (Sura al-Baqara: 164)

A person so disposed recognizes the signs of God's existence everywhere he looks, perceiving Him for His true might. Believers keep their minds continually occupied with remembrance of God, while the majority of humanity spend their lives without a thought to these facts. In a verse of the Qur'an, the ideal behaviour of a Muslim is related as follows:

...Those who remember God, standing, sitting and lying on their sides, and reflect on the creation of the heavens and the earth: "Our Lord, You have not created this for nothing. Glory be to You! So safeguard us from the punishment of the Fire." (Sura Al 'Imran: 191)

GOD'S INFINITE GREATNESS AND POWER

God created the order of the universe in superb detail to allow man to grasp His greatness. A verse referring to this order reads, "...so that you might know that God has power over all things and that God encompasses all things in His knowledge." (Sura at-Talaq: 12). Faced with the sublimity of the details of this order, man becomes in awe, recognizing that God's wisdom, knowledge and might is infinite.

So expansive is God's knowledge that what for us is "infinite" is in His sight already ended. Every event that has taken place since the creation of time, until deep into eternity, was predetermined and ended in God's sight. (See *Timelessness and The Reality of Fate*, by Harun Yahya) This is related in the Qur'an as follows:

We have created all things in due measure. Our command is only one word, like the blinking of an eye. We destroyed those of your kind in the past. But is there any rememberer there? Everything they did is in the Books. Everything is recorded, big or small. (Sura al-Qamar: 49-53)

Man must seek to appreciate the extent of God's knowledge, and reflect to comprehend His greatness.

Billions of people have appeared on earth since time immemorial. Therefore, God created billions of pairs of eyes, billions of different fingerprints, billions of different eye tissues, billions of different types of humans... If He so willed, He could also create billions more. As stated in the Qur'an, **"...He adds to creation in any way He wills. God has power over all things."** (Sura Fatir: 1)

God also possesses the power to create many other things beyond our limited imagination. The entire extent of the treasures God has bestowed in this world for His servants is all within His sight. He sends down to us only that which He wills, all within a measure predetermined:

There is nothing that does not have its stores with Us and We only send it down in a known measure. (Sura al-Hijr: 21)

This matter, manifested everywhere in God's superb creation, holds true for both that which we know as well as that which we do not. To this, God draws attention in the verse, **"...and He creates other things you do not know."** (Sura an-Nahl: 8) He creates many other things of which we are entirely unaware.

God has created many worlds and beings which we cannot see. To better understand the possibility of the existence of other worlds, we should consider the following: a picture is two dimensional–width and length. The world in which we live, however, is 3 dimensional–width, length and depth–(time can be considered as the 4th dimension). The rest is beyond our comprehension. However, in the sight of God, there are other dimensions. Angels, for instance, are beings that live in another dimension. According to the Qur'an, angels can see and hear us from the dimension and space in which they exist. Furthermore, the two angels, seated on our either shoulder, each, and at every moment, is recording every word we speak and every deed we do. Yet, we do not see them. Jinn are also beings of another dimension, as we are informed by the Qur'an. They, like us human beings, are also tested, all through their lives, and will ultimately be brought before judgement by God. However, they are possessed of completely different attributes than humans; their existence is dependent upon an entirely different system of cause and effect.

These are all facts that deserve careful consideration in order to attain a better grasp of God's splendid creation. It is within God's power to create innumerable new worlds, beings and situations. Furthermore, each is He able to create with a limitless degree of differentiation. Indeed, in a nature unknown to us, God will create Paradise and Hell. While systems left to their own in this world tend to age, become corrupted, and eventually expire, in Paradise, unaffected by the passage of time, nothing will deteriorate; **"rivers** of milk whose taste will never change" is an example to elucidate this feature of Paradise. The human body too will not degenerate; nor will anything ever age. According to the Qur'an, everyone in Paradise will be of like age, will live together for all eternity, in the best condition, and without growing older or losing their beauty. God also informs us in the Qur'an that in it will be bursting springs for us from which to drink. Hell, on the other hand, will be utterly different; in it, God will create unimaginable torment. No one will be able to conceive the pain of such torment until he experiences it.

On everything in this world, God has placed a limit. Everything has a finite existence. This being the case, in order to comprehend "eternity," and God's infinite might, we need to exercise our minds and compare these ideas with something that is familiar. We can only come to know to the extent that God permits us. God, however, is infinite in knowledge. Let us consider the following example, God has created 7 basic colours. It is impossible for us to visualize another colour. (The case is similar to describing the colour red to someone who is blind by birth; no description would be adequate.) However, God is able to create more than these basic colours. Although, unless He so wills, we will never be able to have a grasp that which is beyond what He has willed for us to know.

All that we have just mentioned belongs to that knowledge that God has allotted us in this world. But, one point deserves particular attention; because God's power and might is infinite, anything can happen, and at any time, by His will. God's Messenger, the Prophet Muhammad (Pbuh) also referred to the eternal power of God when he said, *"The seven heavens and the seven earths are no more in God's Hand than a mustard seed in the hand of one of you."* God explains the infiniteness of His knowledge in the

Qur'an as follows:

> If all the trees on earth were pens and all the sea, with seven more seas besides, was ink God's words still would not run dry. God is Almighty, All-Wise. (Sura Luqman: 27)

In brief, no matter how hard we strive to do so, we cannot possibly come to grasp the extent of God's knowledge, because it is unlimited. We can comprehend it only as far as God permits us to do so:

> God, there is no god but Him, the Living, the Self-Sustaining. He is not subject to drowsiness or sleep. Everything in the heavens and the earth belongs to Him. Who can intercede with Him except by His permission? He knows what is before them and what is behind them but they cannot grasp any of His knowledge save what He wills. His Footstool encompasses the heavens and the earth and their preservation does not tire Him. He is the Most High, the Magnificent. (Sura al-Baqara: 255)

LOVE OF GOD AND FEAR OF GOD

God says, "Do not take two gods. He is only One God. So dread Me alone." (Sura an-Nahl: 51)

Fear of God is one of the essential attributes of a believer. Because, it is fear of God that draws a person nearer to God, makes him attain a deeper faith, enables him to conduct himself responsibly towards God every moment of his life, and nurtures his dedication to values of the Qur'an. The fact that the good morals God expects from His servants come with the fear of God is reaffirmed by the Prophet Muhammad (Pbuh) in these words:

Fear God wherever you are; if you follow an evil deed with a good one you will obliterate it; and deal with people with a good disposition. (At-Tirmidhi)

Failure to understand the real meaning of fear of God causes some to confuse it with other kinds of mundane fears. However, fear of God differs greatly from all other types of fear.

The Arabic word used in the original text of the Qur'an (khashyat) expresses overwhelming respect. On the other hand, the Arabic word used in the Qur'an to refer to worldly fears (Khawf) expresses a simple kind of fear, as in the fear one feels when faces with a wild animal.

A consideration of the attributes of God leads to a better understanding of these two kinds of fear, both expressed by different words in Arabic. Worldly fears are usually caused by a potential threat. For example, one may fear being murdered. However, God is the All-Compassionate, the Most Merciful and the Most Just. Therefore, fear of God implies showing respect to Him, the All-Compassionate, the Most Merciful and the Most Just, and avoiding exceeding His limits, rebelling Him and being of those who deserve His punishment.

The consequences that a fear of God has on people make this difference apparent. Faced with a deadly danger, a person panics; seized with hopelessness and desperation, he fails to exercise his reason and discover a solution. Fear of God, however, actuates wisdom and adherence to one's conscience. Through fear of God, a person is motivated to avoid that which is evil, corruptive, and likely to cause either physical or mental harm to him. Fear of God fosters wisdom and insight. In a verse of the Qur'an, God informs us that it is through fear of God that wisdom and understanding is acquired:

You who believe! If you have fear of God, He will give you a criterion (by which to judge between right and wrong) and erase your bad actions from you and forgive you. God's favour is indeed immense. (Sura al-Anfal: 29)

Worldly fears cause man anxiety. Fear of God, however, not only gives rise to increased spiritual strength, but also to peace of mind.

It is through fear of God that man avoids those evil actions displeasing God. A verse of the Qur'an states, "**...God does not love anyone vain or boastful.**" (Sura an-Nisa': 36). A God-fearing person strives diligently to abstain from boasting, and to engage rather in actions to earn God's love. For that reason, fear of God and love of God are mutually exclusive.

Fear of God, in fact, removes the obstacles to drawing nearer to God and earning His love. Foremost of these obstacles is one's lower self. From the Qur'an, we learn that there are two aspects of the soul; the one inspiring evil and mischief, and the other, guarding against every inclination to evil.

...the self and what proportioned it and inspired it with depravity and a fear of God, he who purifies it has succeeded, he who covers it up has failed. (Sura ash-Shams: 7-10)

Struggling against this evil, and not giving in it, requires spiritual strength. This strength derives from fear of God. A God-fearing person is not enslaved by the selfishness of his soul. The awe he feels for God draws him away from thoughts and deeds unworthy of His pleasure. A verse of the Qur'an informs us that only those who fear God will take heed of the warnings imparted to them:

> You can only warn those who act on the Reminder and fear the All-Merciful in the Unseen. Give them the good news of forgiveness and a generous reward. (Sura Ya Sin: 11)

Man's striving must be to feel a more profound fear of God. To effect this noble sentiment, he must reflect upon God's creation and recognize the supreme artistry and power represented in its every detail. His thinking must enable him to attain a better grasp of His grandeur and add to his awe. Indeed, God commands us:

> You who have faith! Have fear of God with the fear due to Him and do not die except as Muslims. (Sura Al 'Imran: 102)
>
> So have fear of God, as much as you are able to, and listen and obey and spend for your own benefit. It is the people who are safe-guarded from the avarice of their own selves who are successful. (Sura at-Taghabun: 16)

The more a believer fears God, the more loving he becomes. He better acknowledges the beauty of God's creation. He acquires the ability to recognize the multitude of people, nature, animals, and in everything around him, as reflections of God's sublime attributes. Consequently, he comes to feel a deeper love for such blessings, as well as for God, their Creator.

A person who grasps this secret also knows what love of God is. He loves God, over and above anything else, and understands that all beings are the work of His creation. He loves them in accordance with God's pleasure. He loves believers who are submissive to Him, but feels aversion for those who are rebellious towards Him.

The true love that makes man happy, brings him joy and peace, is love of God. Other forms of love, felt for beings other than God, are, in the words of the Qur'an, love peculiar to idolaters, and consistently leads to anguish, sorrow, melancholy and anxiety. The idolaters' love and the love believers feel for God are compared in a verse as follows:

> Some people set up equals to God, loving them as they should love God. But those who believe have greater love for God... (Sura al-Baqara: 165)

THE QUR'AN IS A GUIDE

> That is the Book, without any doubt. It contains guidance for those who have fear of God (Sura al-Baqara: 2)

The Qur'an is the word of God. God has revealed the Qur'an to introduce Himself, to communicate people the purpose of their existence, inform them of the nature of this life, the basis of the test put to them in this world, and their responsibilities towards their Creator, to give them the good news of the hereafter, and describe what constitutes good morals. The Qur'an was revealed by Gabriel to the Prophet Muhammad (Pbuh). Immune to any possible distortion, it is a Book by which people will be held to account on the Day of Judgement. In one verse, God informs us that the Qur'an is under His protection:

> It is We Who have sent down the Reminder and We Who will preserve it. (Sura al-Hijr: 9)

The unique style of the Qur'an, and the supreme wisdom of its teachings, is clear evidence of its being the word of God. This aside, the Qur'an has many miraculous attributes, certifying that it is the revelation of God. A number of scientific discoveries, that could only be attained in the 20th and 21st centuries, were declared in the Qur'an 1400 years ago. This information, that was impossible to verify scientifically at the time of the Qur'an's revelation, has proved once again that it is the word of God.

Another important characteristic of the Qur'an is that–contrary to the Torah and the Gospel–it contains no contradiction whatsoever. This is yet further evidence that it is the word of God. God reminds humanity of this fact as follows:

Will they not ponder the Qur'an? If it had been from other than God, they would have found many inconsistencies in it. (Sura an-Nisa': 82)

The Qur'an is guidance for mankind. It is also the definitive criterion by which to distinguish right from wrong, for which reason another name of the Qur'an is "Furqan," that is "Discrimination":

...He has sent down the Furqan (the Standard by which to discern the true from the false). Those who reject God's Signs will have a terrible punishment... (Sura Al 'Imran: 4)

The Qur'an is a book that admonishes humanity:

This is a communication to be transmitted to mankind so that they may be warned by it and so that they will know that He is One God and so that the wise will pay heed. (Sura Ibrahim: 52)

The Qur'an is the final revelation from God, and will remain until the Day of Judgement. Although the Torah and the Gospel were true scriptures at the time they were revealed, they have lost the quality of their authenticity, because of the reasons explained earlier. God informs us that, in His sight, Islam is the only religion:

If anyone desires anything other than Islam as a religion, it will not be accepted from him, and in the hereafter he will be among the losers. (Sura Al 'Imran: 85)

BELIEF IN THE BOOKS REVEALED BY GOD AND BELIEF IN HIS MESSENGERS

Since the time the Prophet Adam (May be in peace) was sent to the earth, God has sent messengers to every nation, to communicate to them the existence of God and the hereafter, and to convey the divine message. Some of these messengers are those prophets whose names are mentioned in the Qur'an and to whom books were revealed. A Muslim must not discriminate between them, but respect them all equally, since they were all prophets of the same true religion. God commands Muslims to believe in all the prophets, without making distinction:

Say, "We believe in God and what has been sent down to us and what was sent down to Abraham and Ishmael and Isaac and Jacob and the Tribes, and what Moses and Jesus were given, and what all the Prophets were given by their Lord. We do not differentiate between any of them. We are Muslims submitted to Him." (Sura al-Baqara: 136)

The only book by which humanity is responsible in our time is the Qur'an, revealed to the Prophet Muhammad (Pbuh). Because, as the Qur'an informs, the earlier books, which were originally revealed to communicate the truth to mankind, were later altered through additions and deletions:

Woe to those who write the Book with their own hands and then say "This is from God" to sell it for a paltry price. Woe to them for what their hands have written! Woe to them for what they earn! (Sura al-Baqara: 79)

For this reason, Islam was revealed by God as the final religion. God, in a verse of the Qur'an, commands as follows:

...Today I have perfected your religion for you and completed My blessing upon you and I am pleased with Islam as a religion for you... (Sura al-Ma'ida: 3)

The Qur'an also informs us that the Prophet Muhammad (Pbuh) is the last prophet:

Muhammad is not the father of any of your men, but the Messenger of God and the Final Seal of the Prophets. God has knowledge of all things. (Sura al-Ahzab: 40)

Consequently, the only true religion for all times, since the era of the Prophet Muhammad (Pbuh), until the Day of Resurrection, is Islam, and its source, the Qur'an.

FAITH IN THE ANGELS

Angels, as the Qur'an informs us, are the servants of God, who carry out His commands. God has assigned them different duties. Gabriel, for instance, delivers the divine revelation to prophets. There are the angels on each side of a man, writing down whatever he does; angels welcoming people to Paradise, and those angels who are the guardians of the Hell; the angels that take back the souls of men, the angels who assist the believers, the angels who communicate to the messengers, the angels who give the good news of a newborn to the messengers. Angels are obedient beings, who are never arrogant, but who continually glorify God:

> **Everything in the heavens and every creature on the earth prostrates to God, as do the angels. They are not puffed up with pride. (Sura an-Nahl: 49)**

Throughout history, angels have delivered God's messages to mankind. Angels appeared to many prophets, and, in some cases, to sincere believers, such as Mary, and communicated to them the commands and the divine wisdom of God. God informs us about faith in angels in the Qur'an, making it a prerequisite of faith in the Qur'an for Islam. In a verse of the Qur'an, it is stated that faith in angels is an attribute of a believer:

> **The Messenger has faith in what has been sent down to him from his Lord, and so do the believers. Each one has faith in God and His angels and His Books and His Messengers. We do not differentiate between any of His Messengers. They say, 'We hear and we obey. Forgive us, our Lord! You are our journey's end.' (Sura al-Baqara: 285)**

THE TEMPORARY NATURE OF THE LIFE OF THIS WORLD

The life of this world is a trial for humanity. Though God has created countless allurements for man in this world, He has also warned him against becoming overly concerned by them, and forgetting God and His religion. In a verse of the Qur'an, God states that the ostentation of this world is temporary, and that the real pleasure is Paradise, as reward for God's contentment:

> We made everything on the earth adornment for it so that We could test them to see whose actions are the best. (Sura al-Kahf: 7)

> Know that the life of the world is merely a game and a diversion and ostentation and a cause of boasting among yourselves and trying to outdo one another in wealth and children: like the plant-growth after rain which delights the cultivators, but then it withers and you see it turning yellow, and then it becomes broken stubble. In the hereafter there is terrible punishment but also forgiveness from God and His good pleasure. The life of the world is nothing but the enjoyment of delusion. (Sura al-Hadid: 20)

While the believer also enjoys those blessings that are described as the pleasures of this world, unlike the disbeliever, he does not consider them the purpose of his life. He may desire to possess them, but only for the purpose of giving thanks to God, and to use them to earn God's consent. He does not pursue out of greed, because, he knows that that which is of this world is short-lived, just as is his own life. He knows that, after his death, such things will be of no benefit to him. Furthermore, he knows that if he pursues only worldly things, at the expense of nobler goals, for them he sacrifices his hereafter. In a verse of the Qur'an, this important truth is related as follows:

> To mankind the love of worldly appetites is painted in glowing colours: women and children, and heaped-up mounds of gold and silver, and horses with fine markings, and livestock and fertile farmland. All that is merely the

enjoyment of the life of the world. The best homecoming is in the presence of God. (Sura Al 'Imran: 14)

The allure of the things of this world is an essential factor in the test placed upon man in this world. The Satan resorts relentlessly to allurements in his attempts to deceive man. Believers, however, are those people who, though they may be attracted to such allurement, are aware of their true worth. Cognizant that these are the temporary blessings of this world, and that by them they are being tested, the deceptive attraction of these things does not delude them. For this reason, they are not deceived by the Satan, and are able to save themselves from eternal torment. In the Qur'an, God warns mankind as follows:

Mankind! God's promise is true. Do not let the life of the world delude you and do not let the Deluder delude you about God. (Sura Fatir: 5)

On the other hand, those who are without faith, and thus are bereft of wisdom, feel an inner inclination to this world. Under Satan's influence, they make the attainment of the temporary goods of this world the ultimate purpose of their lives. The condition of such people is stated as follows:

No indeed! But you love this fleeting world and you disregard the hereafter. (Sura al-Qiyama: 20-21)

MAN IS BEING TESTED

God has created everything according to His divine wisdom, and has rendered many things to man's service. Clearly, many things in the universe, from the solar system to the ratio of oxygen in the atmosphere, from the animals that provide us meat and milk to water, have been created to serve man. If this fact is recognized to be evident, it follows that it is illogical to think this life has no purpose. Definitely, there is a purpose of this life, explained by God as follows:

> I only created jinn and man to worship Me. (Sura adh-Dhariyat: 56)

Only a minority of humanity understand this purpose of creation and lead their lives thereby. God has granted us life on earth to test whether or not we will conform to this very purpose. Those who sincerely serve God, and those who rebel against Him, will be distinguished from one another in this world. All those blessings (his body, senses, property...) given to man in this world, are a means by which God tests him. In a verse of the Qur'an, God relates the following:

> We created man from a mingled drop to test him, and We made him hearing and seeing. (Sura al-Insan: 2)

Man's duty in this world is to have faith in God and the hereafter, to conduct himself in compliance with the commands of the Qur'an, to observe the limits set by God, and to try to earn His good pleasure. The continuing trials of this life over time reveal those people who are committed to accomplish these tasks. Because God demands a true and sincere faith,—which is the kind of faith that is not attainable only by saying "I believe"—man must demonstrate that he has true faith in God and His religion, and that he will not swerve from the right path despite the cunnings of Satan. Similarly, he must demonstrate that he will not follow the disbelievers, nor prefer the desires of his own self over God's pleasure. His response to the events in his life will reveal all these qualities. God will create certain hardships, during which man must show patience, in order to expose the degree of his dedication to faith in God. This fact is stated in the Qur'an as follows:

Do people imagine that they will be left to say, "We believe," and will not be tested? (Sura al-'Ankabut: 2)

In another verse, God states that those who say, "We believe" will be tested:

Or did you imagine that you were going to enter Paradise without God knowing those among you who had struggled and knowing the steadfast? (Sura Al 'Imran: 142)

This being the case, disappointment in the face of difficulties would not be the right response to allow oneself to have. Such difficulties may be great ordeals or just trivial daily problems. A believer must consider all such circumstances as part of the trial placed upon him, place his trust in God, and conduct himself in compliance with His pleasure. In a verse of the Qur'an, those difficulties placed upon the believers are related as follows:

We will test you with a certain amount of fear and hunger and loss of wealth and life and crops. But give good news to the steadfast. (Sura al-Baqara: 155)

The Prophet Muhammad (Pbuh) also reminded the believers of this, by saying, *"Whoever accepted it [God's trial], will enjoy God's*

Pleasure and whoever is displeased with it, will incur God's Displeasure." (At-Tirmidhi)

Not only will difficulties, but also blessings in this world serve to test man. God tries man with every benefit He bestows upon man, to see whether or not he will be thankful. As well, God creates many circumstances through which man adopt a certain attitude. In the midst of these trials, man may formulate a decision, either in compliance with God's pleasure, or his own soul. If he recognizes such an incident to be a trial from God, and conforms his conduct accordingly to earn God's pleasure, then he succeeds in his test. However, if his decision is in accordance to the dictates of his own soul, it will both be a sin, which he will greatly regret in the hereafter, and a source of anxiety in this world, as it troubles his conscience.

Indeed, God creates everything that happens in this world as a trial. Those events considered to be mere "coincidence" or "bad luck" by the ignorant, are actually circumstances created according to the great subtleties of a divine plan. Of this, God gives the example of Jews who broke the Sabbath, tempted by an abundance of fish:

Ask them about the town which was by the sea when they broke the Sabbath—when their fish came to them near the surface on their Sabbath day but did not come on the days which were not their Sabbath. In this way We put them to the test because they were deviators. (Sura al-A'raf: 163)

The Jews may have thought that the fish came forth to them on a Saturday by "coincidence," but, the event was predetermined as a trial for them by God. As this case makes clear, there is a divine purpose and a test in every occurrence in life. All that befalls a believer has been determined in order that he keep this notion in mind, and that he try to succeed at his test, and adopt a form of behaviour that is in compliance with the consent of God.

DEATH IS NOT THE END

Every self will taste death. We test you with both good and evil as a trial. And you will be returned to Us. (Sura al-Anbiya': 35)

Death, which is certain to happen to all of us, is a very important fact in one's life. We can never know exactly what we will experience in an hour or even in the next moment. This being the case, it is obvious how wrong it would be to plan our lives based on events that may never happen. Death, on the other hand, is the only thing that is certain to happen. Only the recognition of this basic truth makes us understand that we must found our lives according to it. Death is also a part of the trial of man. God informs us in the Qur'an that He created death and life to try man:

He Who created death and life to test which of you is best in action. He is the Almighty, the Ever-Forgiving. (Sura al-Mulk: 2)

Death is the end of merely the life of this world–thus the end of the trial—and the beginning of the next life. For this reason, believers have no fear of death. The thought of death does not distress them, because, every moment of their lives is spent in the pursuit of good deeds as preparation for the hereafter. For disbelievers, however, fear causes them great distress, because they consider it a complete annihilation. Thus, they avoid all thought of death. But it is futile. No soul can escape death when the predetermined time for it has come. This, in a verse, is stressed as follows:

> **Wherever you are, death will catch up with you, even if you are in impregnable fortresses...(Sura an-Nisa': 78)**

To avoid the thought of death is to avoid the truth. As death will eventually catch up with man sooner or later, it is wise to conduct oneself with a mind busy with the thought of death. This is the rational disposition by which believers abide. Until death comes upon them, they engage in good deeds, as God commands us in the Qur'an:

> **And worship your Lord until what is Certain comes to you. (Sura al-Hijr: 99)**

Thinking about death strengthens one's spirit and will. It prevents one's lower soul from leading him astray, by being lured through the false temptations of this world. It instils him with the resolve and determination to avoid all forms of behaviour unpleasing to God. It is for this reason that a believer must often think about death, never forgetting that all people, including himself, will someday die.

From the Qur'an, we learn what really happens to someone who dies, and what he or she actually experiences and feels. When we see someone dying, we only observe his "biological death." The truth is, however, the dying person, though in a totally different dimension, confronts the angels of death. If he is a disbeliever, his death causes him great pain. The angels of death, after extracting his soul, beat and torment him. A disbeliever's trauma is described as follows:

...If you could only see the wrongdoers in the throes of death when the angels are stretching out their hands, saying, "Disgorge your own selves! Today you will be repaid with the punishment of humiliation for saying something other than the truth about God, and being arrogant about His Signs." (Sura al-An'am: 93)

How will it be when the angels take them in death, beating their faces and their backs? That is because they followed what angers God and hated what is pleasing to Him. So He made their actions come to nothing. (Sura Muhammad: 27-28)

On the contrary, death promises great joy and bliss for the believers. Contrary to disbelievers, whose souls are torn from them violently, the souls of believers are drawn from them gently. (Sura an-Nazi'at: 2) This experience is similar to the case of the soul in sleep, which leaves the body and moves into a different dimension (Sura az-Zumar: 42).

Gardens of Eden which they enter, with rivers flowing under them, where they have whatever they desire. That is how God repays those who have fear for Him: those the angels take in a virtuous state. They say, "Peace be upon you! Enter Paradise for what you did." (Sura an-Nahl: 31-32)

BELIEF IN THE HEREAFTER

The life of the world is nothing but a game and a diversion. The abode of the hereafter—that is truly Life if they only knew. (Sura al-'Ankabut: 64)

Either reward or punishment awaits man at the end of the trial that is the life of this world. Those who engage in good deeds, and have faith in God, earn the good pleasure of God, and are rewarded with an eternal Paradise. The wicked, those who deny God and transgress His limits, however, deserve Hell, where they will encounter eternal punishment.

Man never actually disappears. From the very moment we are created, our eternal life begins. That is, we have already started our eternal life. Once our trial has ended, and immediately following the moment of transition, which we call death, we will live on into eternity. Whether that time will be spent in torment or in bliss depends on one's commitment to the Word of God, the Qur'an, and his fastidiousness in observing His limits. This entire system, the universe, the world, human beings, and everything created for human beings, have been designed for an ultimate purpose; the life in the hereafter. God informs us that man's existence in this world is not without a purpose and that, in the hereafter, after his short life in this world, man will have to offer an account of his deeds:

Did you suppose that We created you for amusement and that you would not return to Us? (Sura al-Muminun: 115)

Eternal life is an enormous blessing in comparison to the very short life of the present, which is no more than a "moment". It is truly a great mercy that, in return for following those basic inclinations that are natural to a human being—such as having faith and seeking God's approval—, God bestows upon him the reward of eternal life in Paradise:

As for those who believe and do right actions, We will lodge them in lofty chambers in Paradise, with rivers flowing under them, remaining in them timelessly, for ever. How excellent is the reward of those who act. (Sura al-'Ankabut: 58)

The life of the hereafter is important in the sense that it represents the manifestation of God's infinite justice, as well as the provision of His infinite blessings. The hereafter will be the place where everything a man does in this world will be repaid, where justice and compassion will prevail. The absolute justice of the hereafter is described in a verse as follows:

...Say, "The enjoyment of the world is very brief. The hereafter is better for those who have fear. You will not be wronged by so much as the smallest speck." (Sura an-Nisa': 77)

God, Who possesses the might to create everything, can surely create the hereafter:

Does He Who created the heavens and earth not have the power to create the same again? Yes indeed! He is the Creator, the All-Knowing. (Sura Ya Sin: 81)

FAITH IN THE DAY OF JUDGEMENT

"And the Hour is coming without any doubt and God will raise up all those in the graves." (Sura al-Hajj: 7)

The Day of Judgement is the day the duration predestined for this universe comes to an end. That day, the trial placed upon humanity will come to an end, and this world, the arena of this trial, will reduce to nothing. This is the end promised by God in the Qur'an. That the present life of the universe will come to an end is a fact confirmed by scientific observation. In the Qur'an, a number of verses that depict the Day of Judgement are as follows:

> So when the Trumpet is blown with a single blast, and the earth and the mountains are lifted and crushed with a single blow, on that Day, the Occurrence will occur and Heaven will be split apart, for that Day it will be very frail. (Sura al-Haqqa: 13-16)

On the Day of Judgement, God will raise all people who have died:

> Then on the Day of Rising you will be raised again. (Sura al-Muminun: 16)

On that day, God will gather the people and raise them all:

> God, there is no god but Him. He will gather you to the Day of Rising about which there is no doubt. And whose speech could be truer than God's? (Sura an-Nisa': 87)

The Day of Rising is the day when each one will stand in God's presence, and every single deed each engaged in, will be disclosed:

> On that Day you will be exposed–no concealed act you did will stay concealed. (Sura al-Haqqa: 18)

That day, everyone will receive the reward for their deeds, and God will carry out His infinite justice:

We will set up the Just Balance on the Day of Rising and no self will be wronged in any way. Even if it is no more than the weight of a grain of mustard-seed, We will produce it. We are sufficient as a Reckoner. (Sura al-Anbiya': 47)

The Day of Resurrection is that time when God will bring an end to the present existence of the universe, the earth and everything in it. In that moment, God, the Creator of all such laws, will render all present laws ineffective, unleashing a chain of unprecedented disasters beyond one's imagination.

A series of very delicate equilibriums make life possible for us in this world. The distance of the world to the sun, and the speed at which it spins on its axis, are perfectly determined for the sake of man's survival on this planet. The gravitational force, the atmosphere that serves as a ceiling to protect the earth against celestial bodies that may destruct it, and many other similar systems have all been specifically created. It is God, the Lord of all the worlds, Who created these finely tuned equilibriums in order to make life possible, before even man existed. It is God Who sustains the universe at every moment:

God keeps a firm hold on the heavens and earth, preventing them from vanishing away. And if they vanished no one could then keep hold of them. Certainly He is Most Forbearing, Ever-Forgiving. (Sura Fatir: 41)

At that moment when God will disrupt the functioning of these varied delicate equilibriums, everything will perish. That moment will be the Day of Judgement. People whose souls will go through the Day of Judgement will be terrified by the horror of that day:

Mankind, have fear of your Lord! The quaking of the Hour is a terrible thing. On the day they see it, every nursing woman will be oblivious of the baby at her breast, and every pregnant woman will abort the contents of her womb, and you will think people drunk when they are not drunk; it is just that the punishment of God is so severe. (Sura al-Hajj: 1-2)
How will you safeguard yourselves, if you are disbelievers, against a Day which will turn children grey? (Sura al-Muzzammil: 17)

God informs us what other things will happen on the Day of Judgement:

When the sun is compacted in blackness,
when the stars fall in rapid succession,
when the mountains are set in motion,
when the camels in foal are neglected,
when the wild beasts are all herded together,
when the oceans surge into each other,
when the selves are arranged into classes,
when the baby girl buried alive is asked
for what crime she was killed,
when the Pages are opened up,
when the Heaven is peeled away,
when the Fire is set ablaze,
when Paradise is brought up close:
then each self will know what it has done.
(Sura at-Takwir: 1-14)

THE RESURRECTION

He makes likenesses of Us and forgets his own creation, saying, "Who will give life to bones when they are decayed?" Say "He Who made them in the first place will bring them back to life." (Sura Ya Sin: 78-79)

The resurrection is a re-creation of life after death. Death is not the cessation of existence. The world, which God has created to put man to test, will serve to determine his lot in the afterlife. After death, every soul will be re-created in a new body, and begin its life in the hereafter, where God will place him either in Hell or Paradise, depending on his deeds in the world. The resurrection of humanity is easy to accomplish for God. In a verse, the rising of the people all together on the Day of Judgement is described as follows:

It is We Who give life and cause to die and We are their final destination. The Day the earth splits open all around them as they come rushing forth, that is a gathering, easy for Us to accomplish. (Sura Qaf: 43-44)

Some people doubt that God could raise man from the dead. However, it is God Who first created man out of nothing, and therefore, certainly has the power to bring him back to life again. God informs us of this fact in the Qur'an:

Mankind! If you are in any doubt about the Rising, know that We created you from dust then from a drop of sperm then from a clot of blood then from a lump of flesh, formed yet unformed, so We may make things clear to you. We make whatever We want stay in the womb until a specified

time and then We bring you out as children so that you canand then We bring you out as children so that you can reach your full maturity. Some of you die and some of you revert to the lowest form of life so that, after having knowledge, they then know nothing at all. And you see the earth dead and barren; then when We send down water onto it, it quivers and swells and sprouts with luxuriant plants of every kind. That is because God is the Real and gives life to the dead and has power over all things. (Sura al-Hajj: 5-6)

To make an example of this re-creation, God draws our attention to natural phenomena around us. After rainfall, God revives dead, barren soil where nothing could grow so that it becomes productive again. Similarly, bringing man back to life after his death is easy for God:

It is He Who sends out the winds, bringing advance news of His mercy, so that when they have lifted up the heavy clouds, We dispatch them to a dead land and send down water to it, by means of which We bring forth all kinds of fruit. In the same way We will bring forth the dead, so that hopefully you will pay heed. (Sura al-A'raf: 57)

Everything is easy for God. The Qur'an states that the creation or resurrection of humanity is like that of a single person:

Your creation and rising is only like that of a single self. God is All-Hearing, All-Seeing. (Sura Luqman: 28)

THE DAY OF JUDGEMENT

Asking, "When is the Day of Judgement?" (Sura adh-Dhariyat: 12)

What you are promised is certainly true— the Judgement will certainly take place! (Sura adh-Dhariyat: 5-6)

God holds man responsible for his deeds. Every person, who has been tested in this world, will be called to account of his deeds on the Day of Judgement. On that day, he will witness that nothing was kept hidden from God, and his every good or evil deed will be disclosed:

> The Day when they will issue forth and when not one thing about them will be hidden from God. "To whom does the kingdom belong today? To God, the One, the Conqueror! Every self will be repaid today for what it earned. Today there will be no injustice. God is swift at reckoning." (Sura Ghafir: 16-17)

Man does not always receive the punishment he deserves in this world. God grants a time to some, though He informs us that He will pay them in full for all their evil deeds in the hereafter. This being the case, it is unwise that those who commit illicit acts should assume they have evaded punishment, simply because they have escaped the law and thus were not punished in this world. On the Day of Judgement, they will see that man can keep nothing hidden from God. By His name "al Hafiz" (He Who preserves all things in detail), God knows man's every deed and commands His angels keep their record. God informs us of this fact in the Qur'an:

it does not give them any headache
nor does it leave them stupefied.
And any fruit they specify
and any bird-meat they desire.
And dark-eyed maidens
like hidden pearls.
As recompense for what they did.
They will hear no prattling in it nor any word of wrong.
All that is said is, "Peace! Peace!"
And the Companions of the Right:
what of the Companions of the Right?
Amid thornless lote-trees
and fruit-laden acacias
and wide-spreading shade
and outpouring water
and fruits in abundance
never failing, unrestricted.
And on elevated couches
We have brought maidens into being
and made them purest virgins,
devoted, passionate, of like age,
for the Companions of the Right.
A large group of the earlier people
and a large group of the later ones. (Sura al-Waqi'a: 11-40)

While God gives to believers the good news of Paradise, a place of bliss and salvation, with its bounteous blessings, He also lets the disbelievers know that they will be sent to Hell. The Qur'an provides an account of Hell, a place of unbearable torment:

And the Companions of the Left:

what of the Companions of the Left?
Amid searing blasts and scalding water
and the murk of thick black smoke,
providing no coolness and no pleasure.
Before that they were living in luxury,
persisting in immense wrongdoing
and saying, "When we are dead and turned to dust and bones,
shall we then be raised again
or our forefathers, the earlier peoples?"
Say: "The earlier and the later peoples
will certainly all be gathered to the appointment of a specified Day.
Then you, you misguided, you deniers
will eat from the tree of Zaqqum,
filling your stomachs with it
and drink scalding water on top of it,
slurping like thirst-crazed camels.
This will be their hospitality on the Day of Judgement!"
(Sura al-Waqi'a: 41-56)

THE AIM IS TO ATTAIN THE GOOD PLEASURE OF GOD

Say: "I am commanded to worship God, making my religion sincerely His." (Sura az-Zumar: 11)

Once having grasped the extent of God's infinite might, to forget His existence and remain heedless is merely to delude oneself. What God demands from human beings is that they seek to earn His good pleasure as their sole priority in life.

Since it is God Who created man, provided him his sustenance and all other such blessings, and Who promised him eternal life in the hereafter, it would be an act of ingratitude for man to seek the pleasure of others, or the gratification of his own self, as his primary aim. The punishment for such ungratefulness is eternal hellfire.

There are two choices a man can make; he can either found his life on God's good pleasure, and thus earn the reward of His Paradise, or choose the path that leads to Hell. A third option is not available for him. This is clearly expressed in the following verse:

Who is better: someone who founds his building on fear of God and His good pleasure, or someone who founds his building on the brink of a crumbling precipice so that it collapses with him into the Fire of Hell? God does not love wrongdoers. (Sura at-Tawba: 109)

Those values praised in the Qur'an are those founded on purely that which achieves God's pleasure. For example, self-sacrifice, which is pleasing to God, is valid only if the person does not expect anything for it in return, but rather only to attain God's good pleasure. It is related in the Qur'an that believers conduct themselves correctly only to seek God's countenance:

They give food, despite their love for it, to the poor and orphans and captives: "We feed you only out of desire for the Face of God. We do not want any repayment from you or any thanks." (Sura al-Insan: 8-9)

God's Messenger, the Prophet Muhammad (Pbuh) also stated in a hadith that God's Pleasure must always be held above man's pleasure:

Whoever seeks God's Pleasure at the expense of men's displeasure, will win God's Pleasure and God will cause men to be pleased with him. And whoever seeks to please men at the expense of God's Displeasure, will win the Displeasure of God and God will cause men to be displeased with him. (Narrated by Ibn Hibban in his Saheeh)

The greatest honour and gratification man can ever attain is God's good pleasure. God makes His servants pleased with Him through the multitude of blessings He bestows on them. In a verse of the Qur'an, the reward for believers who are pleased with God, and with whom God is pleased, is related as follows:

Their reward is with their Lord: Gardens of Eden with rivers flowing under them, remaining in them timelessly, for ever and ever. God is pleased with them and they are pleased with Him. That is for those who fear their Lord. (Sura al-Bayyina: 8)

God's good pleasure is not only earned solely by performing certain acts of worship at definite times. God's good pleasure is also earned by conducting oneself correctly throughout one's lifetime. The following verse informs us that a believer's entire life must be oriented towards a single goal:

Say: "My prayer and my rites, my living and my dying, are for God alone, the Lord of all the worlds." (Sura al-An'am: 162)

SIN AND REPENTANCE

One of the reasons for people's detachment from the religion is that they consider themselves unforgivable out of the deep distress they feel because of the sins they have committed. Satan attempts repeatedly to instil such despair in human beings. To one who has committed a sin, he stealthily whispers the message, "You are wicked and rebellious against God." If he has committed only a few sins, Satan tempts him to sin still more. Towards his purpose, Satan employs the feeling of embarrassment man feels towards God, but manipulates this feeling in order to draw man further distant from God.

However, like all others, this trick of Satan's is a feeble one. The fact that someone committed a sin does not mean that he has been cursed by God, and that he will never be able to follow the straight path again. Not just one simple sin, but even if he were to commit the greatest sins, over and over again, he will always have the opportunity to repent and turn towards God. God informs us in the Qur'an that He will forgive each person who sincerely repents of his sins, that is, asks for forgiveness and remains firm in not committing the same sin again:

> **But if anyone repents after his wrongdoing and puts things right, God will turn towards him. God is Ever-Forgiving, Most Merciful. (Sura al-Ma'ida: 39)**

God is infinite in mercy. In a verse of the Qur'an, He provides the good news to His servants, "**...I am the Ever-Returning, the Most Merciful**" (Sura al-Baqara: 160). Every individual has the opportunity to repent. God even accepted the repentance of Jews, who went astray and worshipped an idol they made out of gold, after having believed in Him, and forgave them:

> **And when Moses said to his people, "My people, You wronged yourselves by adopting the Calf so turn towards your Maker and kill your own (guilty) selves. That is the best thing for you in your Maker's sight." And He (God) turned towards you. He is the Ever-Returning, the Most Merciful. (Sura al-Baqara: 54)**

After repentance and asking for God's forgiveness, a person may well again become heedless, committing the same sin again. In fact, this may happen many times over. However, provided that that person repents once and for all, and is committed to not sin again, he may hope for God's mercy.

Nevertheless, as it is in every issue, the important factor is sincerity. An insincere action is unacceptable in God's sight. If one is not resolved to ending his sinning, and says, "I will repent eventually," he is clearly insincere, which is likely to bring sorrow to man. God warns those who hold such rationale as follows:

> **God only accepts the repentance of those who do evil in ignorance and then quickly make repentance after doing it. God turns towards such people. God is All-Knowing, All-Wise. There is no repentance for people who persist in doing evil until death comes to them and who then say, "Now I make repentance," nor for people who die disbeliever. We have prepared for them a painful punishment. (Sura an-Nisa': 17-18)**

RELIGION IS IN CONFORMITY WITH THE NATURAL INCLINATION OF MANKIND

So set your face firmly towards the religion, as a pure natural believer, God's natural pattern on which He made mankind... (Sura ar-Rum: 30)

Surely, it is God Who best knows the nature of man, which He has Himself created. This being the case, He is the One Who best knows people's needs and the ways to meet them. From how to maintain one's physical well-being, to how to remain spiritually strong, or how to attain a satisfying social life, are all known to God. For example, a human being, by nature, is attracted to all forms of mercy, love and virtuous conduct. He expects to be treated with mercy and compassion. He detests and avoids injustice, immorality, and all forms of wickedness. He feels so by God's Will. Because, God has instiled these values as part of a human's nature, he likes the good and avoids the wicked.

There are certain basic values in the Qur'an that God commands man to adopt; to be compassionate, merciful, reliable, honest and humble and to avoid tyranny, injustice and wickedness. In other words, that which is demanded by the religion of Islam, which God has revealed to mankind, and what man is naturally inclined to, are like the lock and the key that unlocks it, in perfect harmony with one another. God informs us of this fact in the Qur'an as follows:

So set your face firmly towards the religion, as a pure natural believer, God's natural pattern on which He made mankind. There is no changing God's creation. That is the true religion—but most people do not know it. (Sura ar-Rum: 30)

Unless people observe the limits set by God in the Qur'an, they wrong their own souls. Because, by failing to adopt the values that are in accordance with their creation, they appropriate attitudes against their very nature; this causes anxiety not only in themselves, but also makes them troublesome to society. As here stated:

...God does not wrong people in any way; rather it is people who wrong themselves. (Sura Yunus: 44)

We need to keep in mind that one can only live by the values praised by the religion of Islam if he feels it sincerely, with a heartfelt desire. A religion that is imposed by force is both unacceptable in God's sight, as well as a cause for the proliferation of insincere people, referred to as hypocrites in the Qur'an. This leads to the formation of an undesirable societal structure. God commands that people must not be compelled in the name of religion:

There is no compulsion where the religion is concerned. Right guidance has become clearly distinct from error. Anyone who rejects false gods and has faith in God has grasped the Firmest Handhold, which will never give way. God is All-Hearing, All-Knowing. (Sura al-Baqara: 256)

Consequently, in no realm does the religion of Islam exert pressure on people; on the contrary, it provides the basis upon which true freedom of conscience can be established. A person who adopts the values of the Qur'an can in no way be bound. Since he lives in compliance with his faith of his own accord, and through the exercise of his reason, he always feels contented and at peace.

Those who do not adhere to these religious values, on the other hand, can never attain the freedom believers enjoy, due to the countless norms and traditions that prevail in society. Societies that fail to live according to the values of Islam formulate values and criteria themselves, embracing taboos, and thereby, of their own doing, merely limit the freedom endowed to them by God. This being the case, those who are distant from the religion remain deprived of spiritual freedom, due to inappropriate rules and sanctions the society has imposed on them, as well as the many principles they unnecessarily adopt themselves.

The main force binding man, greater than any law of society, is the corruption of his own soul. Immoderate desires are a source of continual anxiety to him. They foster in him feelings of insecurity and fear of the future. Because of these negative tendencies within himself, he becomes ensnared in a difficult struggle with his various passions and desires. His soul relentlessly commands him to accumulate more assets, to make more money, or to win the admiration of others. Yet, these are all insatiable desires. The desire for wealth is a deep-seated passion, common to many. However, the fulfilment of this desire only arouses further false desires. Essentially, worldly desires always tend to become part of a vicious cycle.

Man can only save himself from such ignorance through faith in God and surrender to Him. As the Qur'an puts it: "**...It is the people who are safe-guarded from the avarice of their own selves who are successful.**" (Sura al-Hashr: 9)

Man attains freedom only when he ceases to be a slave to his passions. From then on, satisfying the endless desires mentioned above finally ceases to be his purpose in life. He begins a life in which earning God's good pleasure becomes his only purpose, the purpose for which God has created him.

This is true freedom; being a servant to God, and thus

liberating oneself from everything other than God. It is for this reason that the wife of Imran prayed thus:

> ...My Lord, I have pledged to You what is in my womb, devoting it to Your service. Please accept my prayer. You are the All-Hearing, the All-Knowing. (Sura Al 'Imran: 35)

For the same reason, Abraham said to his father:

> **Father, why do you worship what can neither hear nor see and is not of any use to you at all? (Sura Maryam: 42)**

Throughout history, the messengers God sent to humanity invited them to save themselves from the corruption of their own souls, or becoming servants to human beings, to serve only God. Only when they save themselves from such perversion, which is against the purpose of their creation, can they find relief. It is for this very reason that God's Messenger (Pbuh) is depicted in the Qur'an as a person who "...relieves people of their heavy loads and the chains which were around them":

> **...those who follow the Messenger, the Unlettered Prophet, whom they find written down with them in the Torah and the Gospel, commanding them to do right and forbidding them to do wrong, making good things lawful for them and bad things unlawful for them, relieving them of their heavy loads and the chains which were around them. Those who believe in him and honour him and help him, and follow the Light that has been sent down with him, they are the ones who are successful.' (Sura al-A'raf: 157)**

Another factor in Islam's conformity with human-nature is its simplicity. God has also made the religion, which He has revealed as a religion in conformity with the creation of the human being, easy to practice. This fact is stressed in various verses:

> **God desires to make things lighter for you. Man was created weak. (Sura an-Nisa': 28)**

Religion Is In Conformity With The Natural Inclination Of Mankind

...God desires ease for you; He does not desire difficulty for you... (Sura al-Baqara: 185)

But as for him who believes and acts rightly, he will receive the best of rewards and We will issue a command, making things easy for him. (Sura al-Kahf: 88)

From a drop of sperm He created him and proportioned him. Then He eases the way for him. (Sura Abasa: 19-20)

This simplicity also holds true for acts of worship. Regarding the rite of fasting, a religious duty observed during the month of Ramadan, God commands the following:

The month of Ramadan is the one in which the Qur'an was sent down as guidance for mankind, with Clear Signs containing guidance and discrimination. Any of you who are resident for the month should fast it. But any of you who are ill or on a journey should fast a number of other days. God desires ease for you; He does not desire difficulty for you. You should complete the number of days and proclaim God's greatness for the guidance He has given you so that hopefully you will be thankful. (Sura al-Baqara: 185)

To conclude, Islam is a religion that is entirely in conformity with the nature of man. Because, it is God Who is pleased with Islam as a religion for man, and it is He Who has created him. God desires not difficulty but ease for His servants, and determined as their religion those values that best conform to their needs, wishes and manner of living. In a verse of the Qur'an, our Lord commands as follows:

...Today disbelievers have despaired of overcoming your religion. So do not be afraid of them but be afraid of Me. Today I have perfected your religion for you and completed My blessing upon you and I am pleased with Islam as a religion for you... (Sura al-Ma'ida: 3)

BELIEVERS MUST BE TOGETHER AND COOPERATE

Hold fast to the rope of God all together, and do not separate. Remember God's blessing to you when you were enemies and He joined your hearts together so that you became brothers by His blessing. You were on the very brink of a pit of the Fire and He rescued you from it. In this way God makes His Signs clear to you, so that hopefully you will be guided... (Sura Al 'Imran: 103)

People generally tend to make friends with others who possess similar qualities of character. They prefer people who share their outlook on life, enjoy the same things, and with whom they can get along well. As a consequence, those who share the same views inevitably build a strong bond among themselves. Honourable and honest people attract honourable and honest people like themselves; they do not make friends with wicked people. People who are dishonest and prone to mischief, on the other hand, tend to associate with others who are dishonest.

Believers, who are the only group, among all others, with whose character God is pleased, must, in accordance to God's command, and in conformity with their natural inclination, always remain together.

Indeed, it is an act of worship commanded by God in the Qur'an. God commands believers to remain together with other believers, and not to obey those who are irreverent:

Restrain yourself patiently with those who call on their Lord morning and evening, desiring His face. Do not turn your eyes from them, desiring the attractions of this world. And

do not obey someone whose heart We have made neglectful of Our remembrance and who follows his own whims and desires and whose life has transgressed all bounds. (Sura al-Kahf: 28)

Believers are the only group of people on earth that seek God's pleasure. Only they adopt the character traits with which God is pleased. These are not sufficient alone, however; it is necessary for there to be an environment where these values may be practiced and people to whom they may be exercised. God wants us to be just, to behave compassionately and mercifully, to enjoin what is right, and to adopt the values praised in the Qur'an. However, one cannot adhere to these values without the existence of other people. In other words, to be a compassionate and self-sacrificing person, one needs to be around the type of people who can appreciate this excellence of character, as well as deserve such treatment. Such people are the believers.

No sincere believer wants to make friends with someone who does not conduct himself as God commands, who has not adopted the values of the Qur'an, and thus, who wants only to be around other thoughtless people like himself. Furthermore, he does not nurture affection towards people who do not respect his beliefs, who condemn him because of his faith in God and his living his life by the values of the religion, and wants to drive him away from society and treat him with hostility:

You who believe! Do not take My enemy and your enemy as friends, showing love for them when they have rejected the truth that has come to you, driving out the Messenger and yourselves simply because you believe in God your Lord. If you have gone forth to strive for My sake and seeking My

pleasure, keeping secret the love you have for them, I know best what you conceal and what you make known. Any of you who do that have strayed from the right way. If they come upon you, they will be your enemies and stretch out their hands and tongues against you with evil intent, and they would dearly love you to become disbelievers. (Sura al-Mumtahana: 1-2)

God informs us that it is not right to harbour love for such people, nor to make friends with them, and adds that believers must always remain with other believers:

You who believe! Have fear of God and be with the truly sincere. (Sura at-Tawba: 119)

Of course, a believer must approach everyone, including disbelievers, with a friendly and tolerant manner, and treat them justly. However, treating disbelievers with tolerance and justice is very different from actually adopting them as close friends. A believer takes only those who are believers like him as friends. This is God's command:

Your friend is only God and His Messenger and those who believe: those who attend to their prayers, pay the welfare tax (zakat), and kneel down in worship. (Sura al-Ma'ida: 55)

THE LAST WORD

The facts described throughout this book are those that are the most important in regard to this life. Because man is a being who was created by God, and will ultimately return to Him, nothing can be more important than knowing God and how to serve Him.

Therefore, you need to pay due attention to these facts, and reconsider your goals in life, and, if necessary, reorient your actions and the direction of your lives in the light of the following facts.

Do you know God, your Creator?

Do you give thanks to Him?

Are you aware of the Book He has sent you as a guide to the true path?

Or, what do you do to live by this Book?

We assure you that these are the most important issues related to your life. All else will pass or perish, but God will remain for all eternity. God's promise too, that is, the Day of Judgement and the hereafter, will exist. You will someday die, and will then be raised again, and called forth to God to give account of your deeds.

Do not forget that both a happy life in this world, and a blissful life in the hereafter, depend on your service to God. This is the reason for which God created you. Surrender yourself to the purpose of your creation, worship Him and turn towards Him.

He is Lord of the heavens and the earth and everything in between them, so worship Him and persevere in His worship. Do you know of any other with His Name? (Sura Maryam: 65)

THE MISCONCEPTION OF EVOLUTION

Darwinism, which seeks to deny the fact of creation in the universe, is nothing but an unscientific fallacy. This theory, which argues that life originated from inanimate matter through coincidences, has been demolished with the recognition that the universe was created by God. It is God Who created the universe and Who designed it down to its smallest detail. Therefore, it is impossible for the theory of evolution, which holds that living beings are not created by God, but are products of coincidences, to be true.

Unsurprisingly, when we look at the theory of evolution, we see that this theory is denounced by scientific findings. The design in life is extremely complex and striking. In the inanimate world, for instance, we can explore how sensitive are the balances which atoms rest upon, and further, in the animate world, we can observe in what complex designs these atoms were brought together, and how extraordinary are the mechanisms and structures such as proteins, enzymes, and cells, which are manufactured with them.

This extraordinary design in life invalidated Darwinism at the end of the 20th century.

We have dealt with this subject in great detail in some of our other studies, and shall continue to do so. However, we think that, considering its importance, it will be helpful to make a short summary here as well.

The Scientific Collapse of Darwinism

Although a doctrine going back as far as ancient Greece, the theory of evolution was advanced extensively in the 19th century. The most important development that made the theory the top topic of the world of science was the book by Charles Darwin titled The Origin of Species published in 1859. In this book, Darwin denied that different living species on the earth were created separately by God. According to Darwin, all living beings had a common ancestor and they diversified over time through small changes.

Darwin's theory was not based on any concrete scientific finding; as he also accepted, it was just an "assumption." Moreover, as Darwin confessed in the long chapter of his book titled "Difficulties of the Theory," the theory was failing in the face of many critical questions.

Darwin invested all his hopes in new scientific discoveries, which he expected to solve the "Difficulties of the Theory." However, contrary to his expectations, scientific findings expanded the dimensions of these difficulties.

The defeat of Darwinism against science can be reviewed under three basic topics:

1) The theory can by no means explain how life originated on the earth.

2) There is no scientific finding showing that the "evolutionary mechanisms" proposed by the theory have any power to evolve at all.

3) The fossil record proves completely the contrary of the suggestions of the theory of evolution.

In this section, we will examine these three basic points in general outlines:

The First Insurmountable Step: The Origin of Life

The theory of evolution posits that all living species evolved from a single living cell that emerged on the primitive earth 3.8 billion years ago. How a single cell could generate millions of complex living species and, if such an evolution really occurred, why traces of it cannot be observed in the fossil record are some of the questions the theory cannot answer. However, first and foremost, of the first step of the alleged evolutionary process it has to be inquired: How did this "first cell" originate?

Since the theory of evolution denies creation and does not accept any kind of supernatural intervention, it maintains that the "first cell" originated coincidentally within the laws of nature, without any design, plan, or arrangement. According to the theory, inanimate matter must have produced a living cell as a result of coincidences. This, however, is a claim inconsistent with even the most unassailable rules of biology.

"Life Comes from Life"

In his book, Darwin never referred to the origin of life. The primitive understanding of science in his time rested on the assumption that living beings had a very simple structure. Since medieval times, spontaneous generation, the theory asserting that non-living materials came together to form living organisms, had been widely accepted. It was commonly believed that insects came into being from food leftovers, and mice from wheat. Interesting experiments were conducted to prove this theory. Some wheat was placed on a dirty piece of cloth, and it was believed that mice would originate from it after a while.

Similarly, worms developing in meat was assumed to be evidence of spontaneous generation. However, only some time later was it understood that worms did not appear on meat spontaneously, but were carried there by flies in the form of larvae, invisible to the naked eye.

Even in the period when Darwin wrote The Origin of Species, the belief that bacteria could come into existence from non-living matter was widely accepted in the world of science.

However, five years after the publication of Darwin's book, Louis Pasteur announced his results after long studies and experiments, which disproved spontaneous generation, a cornerstone of Darwin's theory. In his triumphal lecture at the Sorbonne in 1864, Pasteur said, "Never will the doctrine of spontaneous generation recover from the mortal blow struck by this simple experiment."[1]

Advocates of the theory of evolution resisted the findings of Pasteur for a long time. However, as the development of science unraveled the complex structure of the cell of a living being, the idea that life could come into being coincidentally faced an even greater impasse.

Inconclusive Efforts in the 20th Century

The first evolutionist who took up the subject of the origin of life in the 20th century was the renowned Russian biologist Alexander Oparin. With various theses he advanced in the 1930's, he tried to prove that the cell of a living being could originate by coincidence. These studies, however, were doomed to failure, and Oparin had to make the following confession: "Unfortunately, however, the problem of the origin of the cell is perhaps the most obscure point in the whole study of the evolution of organisms."[2]

Evolutionist followers of Oparin tried to carry out experiments to solve the problem of the origin of life. The best known of these experiments was carried out by American chemist Stanley Miller in 1953. Combining the gases he alleged to have existed in the primordial earth's atmosphere in an experiment set-up, and adding energy to the mixture, Miller synthesized several organic molecules (amino acids) present in the structure of proteins.

Barely a few years had passed before it was revealed that this experiment, which was then presented as an important step in the name of evolution, was invalid, the atmosphere used in the experiment having been very different from real earth conditions.[3]

After a long silence, Miller confessed that the atmosphere medium he used was unrealistic.[4]

All the evolutionist efforts put forth throughout the 20th century to explain the origin of life ended with failure. The geochemist Jeffrey Bada from San Diego Scripps Institute accepts this fact in an article published in Earth Magazine in 1998:

Today as we leave the twentieth century, we still face the biggest unsolved problem that we had when we entered the twentieth century: How did life originate on Earth?[5]

The Complex Structure of Life

The primary reason why the theory of evolution ended up in such a big impasse about the origin of life is that even the living organisms deemed the simplest have incredibly complex structures. The cell of a living being is more complex than all of the technological products produced by man. Today, even in the most developed laboratories of the world, a living cell cannot be produced by bringing inorganic materials together.

The conditions required for the formation of a cell are too great in quantity to be explained away by coincidences. The probability of proteins, the building blocks of cell, being synthesized coincidentally, is 1 in 10^{950} for an average protein made up of 500 amino acids. In mathematics, a probability smaller than 1 over 10^{50} is practically considered to be impossible.

The DNA molecule, which is located in the nucleus of the cell and which stores genetic information, is an incredible databank. It is calculated that if the information coded in DNA were written down, this would make a giant library consisting of 900 volumes of encyclopaedias of 500 pages each.

A very interesting dilemma emerges at this point: the DNA can only replicate with the help of some specialized proteins (enzymes). However, the synthesis of these enzymes can only be realized by the information coded in DNA. As they both depend on each other, they have to exist at the same time for replication. This brings the scenario that life originated by itself to a deadlock. Prof. Leslie Orgel, an evolutionist of repute from the University of San Diego, California, confesses this fact in the September 1994 issue of the *Scientific American* magazine:

It is extremely improbable that proteins and nucleic acids, both of which are structurally complex, arose spontaneously in the same place at the same time. Yet it also seems impossible to have one without the other. And so, at first glance, one might have to conclude that life could never, in fact, have originated by chemical means.[6]

No doubt, if it is impossible for life to have originated from natural causes, then it has to be accepted that life was "created" in a supernatural way. This fact explicitly invalidates the theory of evolution, whose main purpose is to deny creation.

Imaginary Mechanisms of Evolution

The second important point that negates Darwin's theory is that both concepts put forward by the theory as "evolutionary mechanisms" were understood to have, in reality, no evolutionary power.

Darwin based his evolution allegation entirely on the mechanism of "natural selection." The importance he placed on this mechanism was evident in the name of his book: *The Origin of Species, By Means Of Natural Selection...*

Natural selection holds that those living things that are stronger and more suited to the natural conditions of their habitats will survive in the struggle for life. For example, in a deer herd under the threat of attack by wild animals, those that can run faster will survive. Therefore, the deer herd will be comprised of faster and stronger individuals. However, unquestionably, this mechanism will not cause deer to evolve and transform themselves into another living species, for instance, horses.

Therefore, the mechanism of natural selection has no

evolutionary power. Darwin was also aware of this fact and had to state this in his book *The Origin of Species*:

> *Natural selection can do nothing until favourable individual differences or variations occur.*[7]

Lamarck's Impact

So, how could these "favourable variations" occur? Darwin tried to answer this question from the standpoint of the primitive understanding of science in his age. According to the French biologist Lamarck, who lived before Darwin, living creatures passed on the traits they acquired during their lifetime to the next generation and these traits, accumulating from one generation to another, caused new species to be formed. For instance, according to Lamarck, giraffes evolved from antelopes; as they struggled to eat the leaves of high trees, their necks were extended from generation to generation.

Darwin also gave similar examples, and in his book *The Origin of Species*, for instance, said that some bears going into water to find food transformed themselves into whales over time.[8]

However, the laws of inheritance discovered by Mendel and verified by the science of genetics that flourished in the 20th century, utterly demolished the legend that acquired traits were passed on to subsequent generations. Thus, **natural selection fell out of favour as an evolutionary mechanism.**

Neo-Darwinism and Mutations

In order to find a solution, Darwinists advanced the "Modern Synthetic Theory," or as it is more commonly known, Neo-

-Darwinism, at the end of the 1930's. Neo-Darwinism added mutations, which are distortions formed in the genes of living beings because of external factors such as radiation or replication errors, as the "cause of favourable variations" in addition to natural mutation.

Today, the model that stands for evolution in the world is Neo-Darwinism. The theory maintains that millions of living beings present on the earth formed as a result of a process whereby numerous complex organs of these organisms such as the ears, eyes, lungs, and wings, underwent "mutations," that is, genetic disorders. Yet, there is an outright scientific fact that totally undermines this theory: **Mutations do not cause living beings to develop; on the contrary, they always cause harm to them.**

The reason for this is very simple: the DNA has a very complex structure and random effects can only cause harm to it. American geneticist B.G. Ranganathan explains this as follows:

First, genuine mutations are very rare in nature. Secondly, most mutations are harmful since they are random, rather than orderly changes in the structure of genes; any random change in a highly ordered system will be for the worse, not for the better. For example, if an earthquake were to shake a highly ordered structure such as a building, there would be a random change in the framework of the building which, in all probability, would not be an improvement.[9]

Not surprisingly, no mutation example, which is useful, that is, which is observed to develop the genetic code, has been observed so far. All mutations have proved to be harmful. It was understood that mutation, which is presented as an "evolutionary mechanism," is actually a genetic occurrence that harms living beings, and leaves them disabled. (The most common effect of mutation on human beings is cancer). No doubt, a destructive mechanism cannot be an "evolutionary mechanism." Natural selection, on the other hand, "can do nothing by itself" as Darwin also accepted. This fact shows us that there is no "evolutionary mechanism" in nature. Since no evolutionary mechanism exists, neither could any imaginary process called evolution have taken place.

The Fossil Record: No Sign of Intermediate Forms

The clearest evidence that the scenario suggested by the theory of evolution did not take place is the fossil record.

According to the theory of evolution, every living species has sprung from a predecessor. A previously existing species turned into something else in time and all species have come into being in this way. According to the theory, this transformation proceeds gradually over millions of years.

Had this been the case, then numerous intermediary species should have existed and lived within this long transformation period.

For instance, some half-fish/half-reptiles should have lived in the past which had acquired some reptilian traits in addition to the fish traits they already had. Or there should have existed some reptile-birds, which acquired some bird traits in addition to the reptilian traits they already had. Since these would be in a transitional phase, they should be disabled, defective, crippled living beings. Evolutionists refer to these imaginary creatures, which they believe to have lived in the past, as **"intermediate forms."**

If such animals had really existed, there should be millions and even billions of them in number and variety. More importantly, the remains of these strange creatures should be present in the fossil record. In The Origin of Species, Darwin explained:

> If my theory be true, numberless intermediate varieties, linking most closely all of the species of the same group together must assuredly have existed... Consequently, evidence of their former existence could be found only amongst fossil remains.[10]

Darwin's Hopes Shattered

However, although evolutionists have been making strenuous efforts to find fossils since the middle of the 19th century all over the world, no transitional forms have yet been uncovered. All the fossils unearthed in excavations showed that, contrary to the expectations of evolutionists, life appeared on earth all of a sudden and fully-formed.

A famous British paleontologist, Derek V. Ager, admits this fact, even though he is an evolutionist:

> The point emerges that if we examine the fossil record in detail, whether at the level of orders or of species, we find – over and over again – not gradual evolution, but the sudden explosion of one group at the expense of another.[11]

This means that in the fossil record, all living species suddenly emerge as fully formed, without any intermediate forms in between. This is just the opposite of Darwin's assumptions. Also, it is very strong evidence that living beings are created. The only explanation of a living species emerging suddenly and complete in every detail without any evolutionary ancestor can be that this species was created. This fact is admitted also by the widely known evolutionist biologist Douglas Futuyma:

> Creation and evolution, between them, exhaust the possible explanations for the origin of living things. Organisms either appeared on the earth fully developed or they did not. If they did not, they must have developed from pre-existing species by some process of modification. If they did appear in a fully developed state, they must indeed have been created by some omnipotent intelligence.[12]

Fossils show that living beings emerged fully developed and in a perfect state on the earth. That means that **"the origin of species" is, contrary to Darwin's supposition, not evolution but creation.**

The Tale of Human Evolution

The subject most often brought up by the advocates of the theory of evolution is the subject of the origin of man. The Darwinist claim holds that the modern men of today evolved from some kind of ape-like creatures. During this alleged evolutionary process, which is supposed to have started 4-5 million years ago, it is claimed that there existed some "transitional forms" between modern man and his ancestors. According to this completely imaginary scenario, four basic "categories" are listed:
1. Australopithecus
2. Homo habilis
3. Homo erectus
4. Homo sapiens

Evolutionists call the so-called first ape-like ancestors of men "Australopithecus" which means "South African ape." These living beings are actually nothing but an old ape species that has become extinct. Extensive research done on various Australopithecus specimens by two world famous anatomists from England and the USA, namely, Lord Solly Zuckerman and Prof. Charles Oxnard, has shown that these belonged to an ordinary ape species that became extinct and bore no resemblance to humans.[13]

Evolutionists classify the next stage of human evolution as "homo," that is "man." According to the evolutionist claim, the living beings in the Homo series are more developed than Australopithecus. Evolutionists devise a fanciful evolution scheme by arranging different fossils of these creatures in a particular order. This scheme is imaginary because it has never been proved that there is an evolutionary relation between these different classes. Ernst Mayr, one of the most important proponents of the theory of evolution in the 20th century, contends in his book *One Long Argument* that "particularly historical [puzzles] such as the origin of life or of Homo sapiens, are extremely difficult and may even resist a final, satisfying explanation."[14]

By outlining the link chain as "Australopithecus > Homo habilis > Homo erectus > Homo sapiens," evolutionists imply that each of these species is one another's ancestor. However, recent findings of paleoanthropologists have revealed that Australopithecus, Homo habilis and Homo erectus lived at different parts of the world at the same time.[15]

Moreover, a certain segment of humans classified as Homo erectus have lived up until very modern times. Homo sapiens neandarthalensis and Homo sapiens sapiens (modern man) co-existed in the same region.[16]

This situation apparently indicates the invalidity of the claim that they are ancestors of one another. A paleontologist from

The Misconception Of Evolution

Harvard University, Stephen Jay Gould, explains this deadlock of the theory of evolution although he is an evolutionist himself:

> *What has become of our ladder if there are three coexisting lineages of hominids (A. africanus, the robust australopithecines, and H. habilis), none clearly derived from another? Moreover, none of the three display any evolutionary trends during their tenure on earth.*[17]

Put briefly, the scenario of human evolution, which is sought to be upheld with the help of various drawings of some "half ape, half human" creatures appearing in the media and course books, that is, frankly, by means of propaganda, is nothing but a tale with no scientific ground.

Lord Solly Zuckerman, one of the most famous and respected scientists in the U.K., who carried out research on this subject for years, and particularly studied Australopithecus fossils for 15 years, finally concluded, despite being an evolutionist himself, that there is, in fact, no such family tree branching out from ape-like creatures to man.

Zuckerman also made an interesting "spectrum of science." He formed a spectrum of sciences ranging from those he considered scientific to those he considered unscientific. According to Zuckerman's spectrum, the most "scientific"-that is, depending on concrete data-fields of science are chemistry and physics. After them come the biological sciences and then the social sciences. At the far end of the spectrum, which is the part considered to be most "unscientific," are "extra-sensory perception"-concepts such as telepathy and sixth sense-and finally "human evolution." Zuckerman explains his reasoning:

> *We then move right off the register of objective truth into those fields of presumed biological science, like extrasensory perception or the*

interpretation of man's fossil history, where to the faithful [evolutionist] anything is possible - and where the ardent believer [in evolution] is sometimes able to believe several contradictory things at the same time.[18]

The tale of human evolution boils down to nothing but the prejudiced interpretations of some fossils unearthed by certain people, who blindly adhere to their theory.

Technology In The Eye and The Ear

Another subject that remains unanswered by evolutionary theory is the excellent quality of perception in the eye and the ear.

Before passing on to the subject of the eye, let us briefly answer the question of "how we see." Light rays coming from an object fall oppositely on the retina of the eye. Here, these light rays are transmitted into electric signals by cells and they reach a tiny spot at the back of the brain called the centre of vision. These electric signals are perceived in this centre of the brain as an image after a series of processes. With this technical background, let us do some thinking.

The brain is insulated from light. That means that the inside of the brain is solid dark, and light does not reach the location where the brain is situated. The place called the centre of vision is a solid dark place where no light ever reaches; it may even be the darkest place you have ever known. However, you observe a luminous, bright world in this pitch darkness.

The image formed in the eye is so sharp and distinct that even the technology of the 20th century has not been able to attain it. For instance, look at the book you read, your hands with which you hold it, then lift your head and look around you. Have you ever seen such a sharp and distinct image as this one at any other place? Even the most developed television screen produced by the greatest television producer in the world cannot provide such a sharp image for you. This is a three-dimensional, coloured, and extremely sharp image. For more than 100 years, thousands of engineers have been trying to achieve this sharpness. Factories, huge premises were established, much research has been done, plans and designs have been made for this purpose. Again, look at a TV screen and the book you hold in your hands. You will see that there is a big difference in sharpness and distinction. Moreover, the TV screen shows you a two-dimensional image, whereas with your eyes, you watch a three-dimensional perspective having depth.

For many years, ten of thousands of engineers have tried to make a three-dimensional TV, and reach the vision quality of the eye. Yes, they have made a three-dimensional television system but it is not possible to watch it without putting on glasses; moreover, it is only an artificial three-dimension. The background is more blurred, the foreground appears like a paper setting. Never has it been possible to produce a sharp and distinct vision like that of the eye. In both the camera and the television, there is a loss of image quality.

Evolutionists claim that the mechanism producing this sharp and distinct image has been formed by chance. Now, if somebody told you that the television in your room was formed as a result of chance, that all its atoms just happened to come together and make up this device that produces an image, what would you think? How can atoms do what thousands of people cannot?

If a device producing a more primitive image than the eye could not have been formed by chance, then it is very evident that the eye and the image seen by the eye could not have been formed by chance. The same situation applies to the ear. The outer ear picks up the available sounds by the auricle and directs them to the middle ear; the middle ear transmits the sound vibrations by intensifying them; the inner ear sends these vibrations to the brain by translating them into electric signals. Just as with the eye, the act of hearing finalises in the centre of hearing in the brain.

The situation in the eye is also true for the ear. That is, the brain is insulated from sound just like it is from light: it does not let any sound in. Therefore, no matter how noisy is the outside, the inside of the brain is completely silent. Nevertheless, the sharpest sounds are perceived in the brain. In your brain, which is insulated from sound, you listen to the symphonies of an orchestra, and hear all the noises in a crowded place. However, if the sound level in your brain was measured by a precise device at that moment, it would be seen that a complete silence is prevailing there.

As is the case with imagery, decades of effort have been spent in trying to generate and reproduce sound that is faithful to the original. The results of these efforts are sound recorders, high-fidelity systems, and systems for sensing sound. Despite all this technology and the thousands of engineers and experts who have been working on this endeavour, no sound has yet been obtained that has the same sharpness and clarity as the sound perceived by the ear. Think of the highest-quality HI-FI systems produced by the biggest company in the music industry. Even in these devices, when sound is recorded some of it is lost; or when you turn on a HI-FI you always hear a hissing sound before the music starts. However, the sounds that are the products of the technology of the human body are extremely sharp and clear. A human ear never perceives a sound accompanied by a hissing sound or with atmospherics as does HI-FI; it perceives sound exactly as it is, sharp and clear. This is the way it has been since the creation of man.

So far, no visual or recording apparatus produced by man has been as sensitive and successful in perceiving sensory data as are the eye and the ear.

However, as far as seeing and hearing are concerned, a far greater fact lies beyond all this.

To Whom Does the Consciousness that Sees and Hears Within the Brain Belong?

Who is it that watches an alluring world in its brain, listens to symphonies and the twittering of birds, and smells the rose?

The stimulations coming from the eyes, ears, and nose of a human being travel to the brain as electro-chemical nervous impulses. In biology, physiology, and biochemistry books, you can find many details about how this image forms in the brain. However, you will never come across the most important fact about this subject: Who is it that perceives these electro-chemical nervous impulses as images, sounds, odours and sensory events in the brain? There is a consciousness in the brain that perceives all this without feeling any need for eye, ear, and nose. To whom does this consciousness belong? There is no doubt that this consciousness does not belong to the nerves, the fat layer and neurons comprising the brain. This is why Darwinist-materialists, who believe that everything is comprised of matter, cannot give any answer to these questions.

For this consciousness is the spirit created by God. The spirit needs neither the eye to watch the images, nor the ear to hear the sounds. Furthermore, nor does it need the brain to think.

Everyone who reads this explicit and scientific fact should ponder on Almighty God, should fear Him and seek refuge in Him, He Who squeezes the entire universe in a pitch-dark place of a few cubic centimeters in a three-dimensional, coloured, shadowy, and luminous form.

A Materialist Faith

The information we have presented so far shows us that the theory of evolution is a claim evidently at variance with scientific findings. The theory's claim on the origin of life is inconsistent with science, the evolutionary mechanisms it proposes have no evolutionary power, and fossils demonstrate that the intermediate forms required by the theory never existed. So, it certainly follows that the theory of evolution should be pushed aside as an unscientific idea. This is how many ideas such as the earth-centered universe model have been taken out of the agenda of science throughout history.

However, the theory of evolution is pressingly kept on the agenda of science. Some people even try to represent criticisms directed against the theory as an "attack on science." Why?

The reason is that the theory of evolution is an indispensable dogmatic belief for some circles. These circles are blindly devoted to materialist philosophy and adopt Darwinism because it is the only materialist explanation that can be put forward for the workings of nature.

The Misconception Of Evolution

Interestingly enough, they also confess this fact from time to time. A well known geneticist and an outspoken evolutionist, Richard C. Lewontin from Harvard University, confesses that he is "first and foremost a materialist and then a scientist":

It is not that the methods and institutions of science somehow compel us accept a material explanation of the phenomenal world, but, on the contrary, that we are forced by our a priori adherence to material causes to create an apparatus of investigation and a set of concepts that produce material explanations, no matter how counter-intuitive, no matter how mystifying to the uninitiated. Moreover, that materialism is absolute, so we cannot allow a Divine Foot in the door.[19]

These are explicit statements that Darwinism is a dogma kept alive just for the sake of adherence to the materialist philosophy. This dogma maintains that there is no being save matter. Therefore, it argues that inanimate, unconscious matter created life. It insists that millions of different living species; for instance, birds, fish, giraffes, tigers, insects, trees, flowers, whales and human beings originated as a result of the interactions between matter such as the pouring rain, the lightning flash, etc., out of inanimate matter. This is a precept contrary both to reason and science. Yet Darwinists continue to defend it just so as "not to allow a Divine Foot in the door."

Anyone who does not look at the origin of living beings with a materialist prejudice will see this evident truth: All living beings are works of a Creator, Who is All-Powerful, All-Wise and All-Knowing. This Creator is God, Who created the whole universe from non-existence, designed it in the most perfect form, and fashioned all living beings.

> *They said "Glory be to You!*
> *We have no knowledge except what You*
> *have taught us. You are the All-Knowing,*
> *the All-Wise."*
> *(Sura al-Baqara: 32)*

NOTES

1. Sidney Fox, Klaus Dose, *Molecular Evolution and The Origin of Life*, W.H. Freeman and Company, San Francisco, 1972, p. 4.

2. Alexander I. Oparin, *Origin of Life*, Dover Publications, NewYork, 1936, 1953 (reprint), p. 196.

3. "New Evidence on Evolution of Early Atmosphere and Life", *Bulletin of the American Meteorological Society*, vol 63, November 1982, p. 1328-1330.

4. Stanley Miller, *Molecular Evolution of Life: Current Status of the Prebiotic Synthesis of Small Molecules*, 1986, p. 7.

5. Jeffrey Bada, Earth, February 1998, p. 40

6. Leslie E. Orgel, "The Origin of Life on Earth", *Scientific American*, vol. 271, October 1994, p. 78.

7. Charles Darwin, *The Origin of Species by Means of Natural Selection*, The Modern Library, New York, p. 127.

8. Charles Darwin, *The Origin of Species: A Facsimile of the First Edition*, Harvard University Press, 1964, p. 184.

9. B. G. Ranganathan, *Origins?*, Pennsylvania: The Banner Of Truth Trust, 1988, p. 7.

10. Charles Darwin, *The Origin of Species: A Facsimile of the First Edition*, Harvard University Press, 1964, p. 179.

11. Derek A. Ager, "The Nature of the Fossil Record", *Proceedings of the British Geological Association*, vol 87, 1976, p. 133

12. Douglas J. Futuyma, *Science on Trial*, Pantheon Books, New York, 1983. p. 197.

13. Solly Zuckerman, *Beyond The Ivory Tower*, Toplinger Publications, New York, 1970, pp. 75-94; Charles E. Oxnard, "The Place of Australopithecines in Human Evolution: Grounds for Doubt", *Nature*, vol 258, p. 389.

14. "Could science be brought to an end by scientists' belief that they have final answers or by society's reluctance to pay the bills?" *Scientific American*, December 1992, p. 20.

15. Alan Walker, Science, vol. 207, 7 March 1980, p. 1103; A. J. Kelso, *Physical Antropology*, 1st ed., J. B. Lipincott Co., New York, 1970, p. 221; M. D. Leakey, *Olduvai Gorge*, vol. 3, Cambridge University Press, Cambridge, 1971, p. 272.

16. Jeffrey Kluger, "Not So Extinct After All: The Primitive Homo Erectus May Have Survived Long Enough To Coexist With Modern Humans," *Time*, 23 December 1996.

17. S. J. Gould, Natural History, vol. 85, 1976, p. 30.

18 Solly Zuckerman, *Beyond The Ivory Tower*, p. 19.

19. Richard Lewontin, "The Demon-Haunted World," *The New York Review of Books*, January 9, 1997, p. 28.

Also by Harun Yahya

Many people think that Darwin's Theory of Evolution is a proven fact. Contrary to this conventional wisdom, recent developments in science completely disprove the theory. The only reason Darwinism is still foisted on people by means of a worldwide propaganda campaign lies in the ideological aspects of the theory. All secular ideologies and philosophies try to provide a basis for themselves by relying on the theory of evolution.

This book clarifies the scientific collapse of the theory of evolution in a way that is detailed but easy to understand. It reveals the frauds and distortions committed by evolutionists to "prove" evolution. Finally it analyzes the powers and motives that strive to keep this theory alive and make people believe in it.

Anyone who wants to learn about the origin of living things, including mankind, needs to read this book. *The Evolution Deceit* is also available in Italian, Albanian, Spanish, Indonesian, Russian and Serbo-Croat (Bosnian).

When a person examines his own body or any other living thing in nature, the world or the whole universe, in it he sees a great design, art, plan and intelligence. All this is evidence proving God's being, unit, and eternal power.

For Men of Understanding was written to make the reader see and realise some of the evidence of creation in nature. *For Men of Understanding* is also available in French Indonesian, Urdu German and Russian.

People who are oppressed, who are tortured to death, innocent babies, those who cannot afford even a loaf of bread, who must sleep in tents or even in streets in cold weather, those who are massacred just because they belong to a certain tribe, women, children, and old people who are expelled from their homes because of their religion…Eventually, there is only one solution to the injustice, chaos, terror, massacres, hunger, poverty, and oppression: the morals of the Qur'an.

"Everything that constitutes our life is a totality of perceptions received by our soul. The things, people, places and events that make our world and our lives meaningful are like a dream; we perceive them only as images in our brain, and have nothing to do with their truth or reality…"

In the book, which consists of a conversation between four people, the prejudices that prevent people from understanding this great truth are removed, and the misconceptions they have are explained.

How was matter and time created from nothingness? What does the Big Bang theory signify about the creation of the universe? What is the parallelism between Einstein's Theory of Relativity and the Qur'anic verses?

All of these questions are answered in this book. If you want to learn the truths about space, matter, time and fate, read this book.

Fascism and communism, which made humanity suffer dark times, are considered to be opposed ideas. However, these ideologies are fed from the same source, on the grounds of which they can attract masses to their side. This source has never drawn attention, always remaining behind the scenes. This source is the materialist philosophy and its adaptation to nature, which is DARWINISM. The acknowledgment of the scientific invalidity of this theory that serves as a basis for cruel dictators and vicious ideological trends will bring about the end of all these detrimental ideologies. This book is also available in French.

Never plead ignorance of God's evident existence, that everything was created by God, that everything you own was given to you by God for your subsistence, that you will not stay so long in this world, of the reality of death, that the Qur'an is the Book of truth, that you will give account for your deeds, of the voice of your conscience that always invites you to righteousness, of the existence of the hereafter and the day of account, that hell is the eternal home of severe punishment, and of the reality of fate.

Darwin's theory of evolution maintained that all living beings emerged as a result of chance coincidence and thus denied Creation. Yet, scientific developments did not favour the evolutionist standpoint and simply opposed it. Different branches of science like biochemistry, genetics, and palaeontology have demonstrated that the claims that life originated as a result of "coincidences" is foolish. This is a book you will read with pleasure and as it makes explicitly clear why the theory of evolution is the greatest aberration in the history of science.

Darwin said: "If it could be demonstrated that any complex organ existed, which could not possibly have been formed by numerous, successive, slight modifications, my theory would absolutely break down." When you read this book, you will see that Darwin's theory has absolutely broken down, just as he feared it would. A thorough examination of the feathers of a bird, the sonar system of a bat or the wing structure of a fly reveal amazingly complex designs. And these designs indicate that they are created flawlessly by God.

Colours, patterns, spots even lines of each living being existing in nature have a meaning. An attentive eye would immediately recognise that not only the living beings, but also everything in nature are just as they should be. Furthermore, he would realise that everything is given to the service of man: the comforting blue colour of the sky, the colourful view of flowers, the bright green trees and meadows, the moon and stars illuminating the world in pitch darkness together with innumerable beauties surrounding man..... *Allah's Artistry in Colour* is also available in Indonesian Arabic.

The unprecedented style and the superior wisdom inherent in the Qur'an is conclusive evidence confirming that it is the Word of God. Apart from this, there are a number of miracles verifying the fact that the Qur'an is the revelation of God, one of them being that, 1,400 years ago, it declared a number of scientific facts that have only been established thanks to the technological breakthroughs of the 20th century. In this book, in addition to the scientific miracles of the Qur'an, you will also find messages regarding the future. *Miracles of the Qur'an* is also available in Serbo-Croat (Bosnian) and Russian.

Man is a being to which God has granted the faculty of thinking. Yet a majority of people fail to employ this faculty as they should... The purpose of this book is to summon people to think in the way they should and to guide them in their efforts to think. This book is also available in Indonesian.

 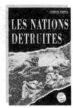 

Many societies that rebelled against the will of God or regarded His messengers as enemies were wiped off the face of the earth completely... *Perished Nations* examines these penalties as revealed in the verses of the Quran and in light of archaeological discoveries. This book is also available in German, French, Spanish, Russian and Portuguese.

These millimeter-sized animals that we frequently come across but don't care much about have an excellent ability for organization and specialization that is not to be matched by any other being on earth. These aspects of ants create in one a great admiration for God's superior power and unmatched creation.

The way to examine the universe and all the beings therein and to discover God's art of creation and announce it to humanity is "science". Therefore, religion adopts science as a way to reach the details of God's creation and therefore encourages science. Just as religion encourages scientific research, so does scientific research that is guided by the facts communicated by religion yield very repid and definite results. This is because religion is the unique source that provides the most correct and definite answer to the question of how the universe and life came into being.

Today, science has proven that the universe was created from nothing with a Big Bang. Moreover, all physical balances of the universe are designed to support human life. Everything from the nuclear reactions in stars to the chemical properties of a carbon atom or a water molecule, is created in a glorious harmony. This is the exalted and flawless creation of God, the Lord of All the Worlds. *The Creation of the Universe* is also available in French.

In this book you will find explanations about eternity, timelessness and spacelessness that you will never have encountered anywhere else and you will be confronted by the reality that eternity has already begun. The real answers to many questions people always ponder such as the true nature of death, resurrection after death, the existence of an eternal life, and the time when all these things will happen are to be found here...

We fall sick many times throughout our lives. When the events of "sickness" and "recovering" take place, our bodies become a battleground in which a bitter struggle is taking place. Microbes invisible to our eyes intrude into our body and begin to increase rapidly. The body however has a mechanism that combats them. Known as the "immune system", this mechanism is the most disciplined, most complex and successful army of the world. This system proves that the human body is the outcome of a unique design that has been planned with a great wisdom and skill. In other words, the human body is the evidence of a flawless creation, which is the peerless creation of God.

In a body that is made up of atoms, you breathe in air, eat food, and drink liquids that are all composed of atoms. Everything you see is nothing but the result of the collision of electrons of atoms with photons.
In this book, the implausibility of the spontaneous formation of an atom, the building-block of everything, living or non-living, is related and the flawless nature of God's creation is demonstrated.

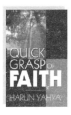

There are questions about religion that people seek answers to and hope to be enlightened in the best way. However in most cases, people base their opinions on hearsay rather than acquiring them from the real source of religion: the Qur'an. In these booklets, you will find the most accurate answers to all the questions you seek answers for and learn your responsibilities towards your Creator.

This book deals with how the theory of evolution is invalidated by scientific findings and experiments in a concise and simple language.

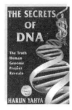

Scientific progress makes it clear that living beings have an extremely complex structure and an order that is too perfect to have come into being by accident. Recently, for example, the perfect structure in the human gene became a top issue as a result of hte completion of the Human Genome Project. In this book, the unique creation of God is once again disclosed for all to see.

Just as a tiny key opens a huge door, this book will open new horizons for its readers. And the reality behind that door is the most important reality that one can come across in one's lifetime. Relating the amazing and admirable features of spiders known by few people and asking the questions of "how" and "why" in the process, this book reveals the excellence and perfection inherent in God's creation.

In the Qur'an, conscience has a meaning and importance beyond its common and everyday use. This book introduces the real concept of conscience that is related in the Qur'an and draws our attention to the kind of understanding, thought, and wisdom that a truly conscientious person has. This book will make you recognise the voice of your conscience and accordingly help you to differentiate it from other sources of inspiration.

God, in the Qur'an, calls the culture of people who are not subject to the religion of God "ignorance." Only a comparison of this culture with the honourable thoughts and moral structure of the Qur'an can reveal its primitive and corrupted nature. The purpose of this book is to take this comparison further, displaying the extent of the "crude understanding" of ignorant societies.

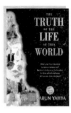

The world is a temporary place specially created by God to test man. That is why, it is inherently flawed and far from satisfying man's endless needs and desires. Each and every attraction existing in the world eventually wears out, becomes corrupt, decays and finally disappears. This is the never-changing reality of life. This book explains this most important essence of life and leads man to ponder the real place to which he belongs, namely the Hereafter.

In the Qur'an, there is an explicit reference to the "second coming of the Jesus to the world" which is heralded in a hadith. The realisation of some information revealed in the Qur'an about Jesus can only be possible by Jesus' second coming…

In the Qur'an, God tells people many secrets. People who are unaware of these secrets experience the trouble and distress caused by this throughout their lives. For those who learn these secrets of the Qur'an, however, the life of this world is very easy, and full of joy and excitement. This book deals with the subjects God related to people as a secret.

The Qur'an has been sent down as a book easily understandable to everyone. Everyone who believes in God and follows his conscience can take counsel from the verses of the Qur'an and obey the commands in the verses. However, those who follow their lower self fail to measure God with His true scale, entertain doubts about the hereafter, interpret the verses of the Qur'an wrongly in their own crooked reasoning. In this book, the reasons why those who do not use their intellect misinterpret the Qur'an are examined and some examples of the unwise interpretations and objections they make concerning the verses are reviewed and answered.

The plan, design, and delicate balance existing in our bodies and reaching into even the remotest corners of the incredibly vast universe must surely have a superior Creator. Man is unable to see his Creator yet he can nevertheless grasp His existence, strength, and wisdom by means of his intellect. This book is a summons to think. A summons to ponder over the universe and living beings and see how they have been created flawlessly. *Allah is Know Through Reason* is also available in Urdu and French.

One of the principal deceptions that impels people into delinquency and makes them pursue their own desires is their heedlessness of death. Both human beings and the universe they live in are mortal. What awaits the disbelievers in the next world is more dreadful: the eternal wrath of hell. This book, based on the verses of the Qur'an, makes a detailed depiction of the moment of death, the day of judgement, and the penalties in hell, and it sounds a warning about the great danger facing us. *Death Resurrection Hell* is also available in Polish.

The purpose of this book is to warn people against the day on which they will say "If only we did not rebel against God. If only we listened to the messengers…" and therefore feel deep regret. This is a summons to live for the cause of God when there is still time. *Before You Regret* is also available in French.

If a person is recently introduced to Islam, many questions may cross his mind since he has just quit the society of ignorance and has not yet learned the faculty to think according to the Qur'an. Answers from the Qur'an aims to reply these questions substantially according to the principles

While watching television or reading the paper, you see many items which you do would not like to see or hear: destitute people, murders, quarrels, ill-treatment, and much more... Certainly, you, too, would like to live in a peaceful and secure society where people live in harmony and friendship. This book is a summons to those who want goodness to prevail: it calls on them to do goodness and to form an alliance with other good people like themselves.

This book maintains that the source of the scourge of terrorism does not come from a divine religion, and that there is no room for terrorism in Islam. It is revealed, in the light of the verses of the Koran and with examples from history, that Islam forbids terrorism and aims to bring peace and security to the world.

The purpose of this book is to display the miraculous features of plants and hence to make people see "the creation miracle" in things they often encounter in the flow of their daily lives and sidestep. Reading and understanding this book will be an important step in coming to an understanding of one's Creator.

Moses is the prophet whose life is most narrated in the Qur'an. The Qur'an provides a very detailed account of his struggle with Pharaoh, the unfavourable conduct of his people and the way the Prophet Moses summoned them to the way of God. This book provides a thorough examination into the life of the Prophet Moses in the light of the Qur'anic verses.

In societies distant from religion, right is often presented as wrong, and vice versa. Unbecoming behaviour which will not please God may be favoured and encouraged. Romanticism is one of those wrong sentiments which is assumed to be "right". This book reveals what a serious threat romanticism – which is imagined to be a simple character trait – poses to societies and individuals, and shows how easy it is to eliminate this danger.

The content of this book is an extremely important truth that astounded large numbers of people, and caused their outlook on life to change drastically. We can sum up this reality like this: "All events, people, buildings, cities, cars, places, which are a part of our life in this world, in short, everything we see, hold, touch, smell, taste and hear, are actually illusions and sensations that form in our brain."

Fascism is an ideology that has brought great disasters to humanity. Not only has it caused millions of people to be killed and tortured simply because of their race, but it has also attempted to abolish all human values. The main purpose of the book is to present various fascist tendencies which appear under different methods and guises, and expose their real origins and objectives. The book also attempts to tear down the mask of fascism, and reveal that fascism is definitely an anti-religionist system.

A study that examines and seeks to remind us of the basic moral principles of the Qur'an, particularly those that are most likely to be forgotten or neglected at times.

The Qur'an has been revealed to us so that we may read and ponder. The Basic Concepts of the Qur'an is a useful resource prepared as a guide to thinking. Some basic Islamic concepts like the soul, conscience, wisdom, loyalty, submission to God, brotherhood, modesty, prayer, patience, are discussed in the light of Qur'anic verses. This book is also available in Portuguese.

Children!
Have you ever asked yourself questions like these: How did our earth come into existence? How did the moon and sun come into being? Where were you before you were born? How did oceans, trees, animals appear on earth? How does a little tiny bee know how to produce delicious honey? How can it build a honeycomb with such astonishingly regular edges? Who was the first human being? In this book you will find the true answers to these questions.

The most serious mistake a man makes is not pondering. It is not possible to find the truth unless one thinks about basic questions such as "How and why am I here?", "Who created me?", or "Where am I going?." Failing to do so, one becomes trapped in the vicious circle of daily life and turns into a selfish creature caring only for himself. *Ever Thought About the Truth?* summons people to think on such basic questions and to discover the real meaning of life. This book is also available in French.

Children's Books

These books, prepared for kids, are about the miraculous characteristics of the living things on the Earth. Full colour and written in a concise style, these books give your children the opportunity to get to know God and His perfect artistry in creation. The World of Our Little Friends: The Ants is also available in Russian and French. Honeybees that Build Perfect Combs is also available in French.